What Maastricht Means for Business

Opportunities and Regulations in the EC Internal Market

BRIAN ROTHERY

Gower

Published by
Gower Publishing
Gower House
Croft Road
Aldershot
Hampshire GU11 3HR
England

Gower
Old Post Road
Brookfield
Vermont 05036
USA

British Library Cataloguing in Publication Data

Rothery, Brian
    What Maastricht Means for Business:
    Opportunities and Regulations in the EC
    Internal Market
    I. Title
    341.2422

    ISBN 0-566-07430-3 hardback
    ISBN 0-566-07431-1 paperback

Typeset in 10/13 Trump Mediaeval by Keyboard Services, Luton
Printed in Great Britain at the University Press, Cambridge

Contents

Preface   ix

Part I   The New Union   1

1   The European Union   3

2   Citizenship and Free Movement   8

3   Uniformity of Law   16

4   Economic and Monetary Union   26
    The UK position   29
    Economic union   29

Part II   The Opportunities   **31**

5 The Public Procurement Market   **33**
The actual public procurement measures   36
New rules on tendering   38
Public works   40
Public supplies   40
The so-called excluded sectors   41
Services   41
The review procedures   42

6 Public Works   **43**
Group 500   44
The authorities subject to the legislation   45
The technical specifications   46
Tendering procedures   47
Time limits for tenders   49
The rules for selection   49

7 Public Supplies   **53**
Tendering procedures   55
The rules for selection of contractors   58
Provision of information   59
A useful timetable   59

8 The EC Market for Services   **62**

9 EC Grants   **67**
Contract research with cost sharing   70
Concentration of research activities   70
The Community's own research   71
Bursaries and subsidies   71
Staying in touch   71
The model contract   74
Details of Framework programmes   75
Conclusion   81

10 Opportunities for Small and Medium-sized Enterprises   **82**
Outsourcing   86
Opportunities for small and medium-sized enterprises   88

11 Selling to the Multinational Corporations   **99**
Advanced manufacturing technology (AMT)   103
Computer integrated manufacturing (CIM)   104
Just in time (JIT)   104
Electronic data interchange (EDI)   105

12 Training Opportunities   **107**

13 Investing in Europe   **112**

Part III   The Tighter Regulations   **117**

14 European Standardization   **119**
ISO and IEC – general background notes   122
Products covered by EC directives   123

15 Products Needing Standards   **124**
Products and processes needing certification   127
Compulsory standards   127
The CE Mark   129
Quality management systems standards   129

16 Product Liability and Consumer Protection   **133**

17 ISO 9000   **139**

18 The Health and Safety Regulations   **145**

19 Environmental Management Standards   **150**
The eco-management and auditing scheme regulation   150
Air emissions   156
Water resources   156
Water supplies and sewage treatment   156
Waste   157
Nuisances   158
Noise   159
Radiation   159
Amenities, trees and wildlife   160
Urban renewal/site dereliction   161
Physical planning   161

Environmental impact assessment   161
Product use   162
Packaging   163
Materials   163
Energy   163
Public safety   164
Health and safety   164

20 Packaging and the Environment   165

21 General Legal Liability   168
Environment impairment liability (E12) insurance
coverage in Europe   173

Part IV   The Infrastructure   177

22 Trans-European Networks and Information Databases 179

23 The Electronic Marketplace   187

24 Testing and Certification   193

25 Other Supports Available to Small
and Medium-sized Enterprises   205

26 Banking Facilities   221
Trade development service   222
Economic information service   223
Foreign currency accounts   223
International money transfer services   224
Export finance   225
Exchange rate services   226
Letters of credit   227

APPENDIX 1   Sample Life-of-programme Agreement   229

APPENDIX 2   Customs, Excise and VAT   246

APPENDIX 3   Other EC Programmes   253

Index   259

Preface

As this book was being written, dramatic events were taking place in Europe. Just before going to press, the Danes ratified the Maastricht Treaty. In the dialogue following the ratification, senior officials in the European Commission were asked what lessons had been learned from the months of doubt and argument in Denmark, UK and elsewhere. One reply was that much more work needed to be done to explain to the people of the emerging union what the Maastricht Treaty really means to them.

A glance at the Contents of this book will give some small indication of the enormous size of that task, and this book is aimed just at people doing business in the internal market. It is hoped that the book will contribute to the process of understanding what the new union means, and that other devices and channels of communication will emerge also.

Both publisher and author have tried to produce the book in the shortest time frame that has been practical, but the reader will need to be sympathetic to the fact that some of the programmes discussed, especially the EC Framework programmes, are changing all the time. Most of the information in the book, however, should not be out of date before the next revision.

This book would have been impossible to write without help and information from many people and companies. These have been acknowledged as far as possible in the text. Above all, however, thanks is due to the Commission of the European Communities, which makes information widely available through friendly staff in its European Commission offices and other information centres throughout Europe.

Brian Rothery
May 1993

PART I

The New Union

CHAPTER 1

The European Union

On 1 January 1993, the Treaty on European Union, or, as it is more popularly known, the Maastricht Treaty of 1992, became a reality. The internal frontiers between the twelve member countries of this new union were dissolved and the single, or internal, market was established. This huge market of over 340 million people is also augmented by its membership of the European Economic Area, which adds the seven EFTA, European Free Trade Association, countries and their 32 million people to its totals. The free trade agreement with EFTA is almost as comprehensive as the rules governing trade within the single market. EFTA comprises the non-EC Scandinavian countries, Switzerland, Austria, Iceland and Lichtenstein.

The European Union, with this great free market of almost 400 million people, and embracing several of the world's leading nations, may now become the most economically powerful entity in the world, and it will complement the powerful economies of North America and the Pacific Rim.

The European Union, created by the Maastricht Treaty, completed and formalized much that was already happening and had happened. Many of the important economic changes had already been set in train for 1993 by the Single European Act. The union is a new stage in the process of integration. It is based on the existing European Community, or EC, and it adds provisions for common foreign and security policies, as well as interior and justice policies.

The Maastricht Treaty, however, also marked the commencement of the single market, many of the business implications of which owe more to previous developments than to the treaty. Examples would include the harmonization of standards and the opening up of public procurement across the twelve member states. This book will cover all of these developments, whether brought into being by the Maastricht Treaty itself, or simply formalized by it. However, let us first deal with the treaty itself.

The Maastricht Treaty represents what the Community itself represents – a good idea, a stage in the process of European integration which began with the establishment of the 'Common Market'. Within its formal charter there are the hopes of ending the division of the European continent and of constructing a new Europe, of deepening the solidarity between peoples, and enhancing the democracies and efficient functioning of institutions, by creating 'a single institutional framework'. There are resolutions to achieve the strengthening and convergence of the economies of the twelve member states, and to establish an economic and monetary union, including a single currency, to establish a common citizenship, to implement a common foreign policy, and to create 'an ever closer union among the peoples of Europe, in which decisions are taken as closely as possible to the citizen'.

The treaty reaffirms the objective of facilitating the free movement of persons, and expresses the determination to promote economic and social progress for all the people of the union, within the context of the accomplishment of the internal market 'and of reinforced cohesion and environmental protection'. The last words, more than any, illustrate the two aspects of the union of most interest to us in this book: opportunities, as in the provisions on cohesion, and regulations as in those on environment.

The internal market consists of opportunities and regulations. One could describe it as a wonderful new world of freedom, where the internal borders and customs posts have been swept away, but where new regulations abound, particularly those covering health and safety, environment, workers' rights, product liability, and certification. There is freedom if you stay out of business, and particularly if you neither manufacture nor distribute goods.

Balancing this is a world of opportunity, where there is a real spirit of doing business across former frontiers, the elimination of what was a vast bureaucracy of customs and product certification, and the huge, liberated public procurement market.

So what is the European Union? In practice it is the EC, or European Community, as it now stands, supplemented by the common policies on foreign affairs, security and justice. It is also an aspiration to act as a united Europe in dealings with the rest of the world. Its Council is the ministers of the twelve member states, and the administration of business and the implementation of policies are carried out by the Commission, which we also call the 'EC'. In addition to the Council of Ministers, there is a European Council which, meeting at least twice a year, consists of the heads of state or government of the twelve member states, assisted by ministers of foreign affairs and the Commission.

For the purposes of this book, the most significant element in the union is the European Community. Article 6 of the treaty finally changes the name of the European Economic Community (EEC) to European Community (EC). The treaty sets the task of the EC or 'Community' as it is called as follows:

> The Community shall have as its task, by establishing a common market and an economic and monetary union and by implementing the common policies or activities referred to in Articles 3 and 3A (see below), to promote throughout the Community a harmonious and balanced development of economic activities, sustainable and non-inflationary growth respecting the environment, a high degree of convergence of economic performance, a high level of employ-ment and of social protection, the raising of the standard of living and quality of life, and economic and social cohesion and solidarity between Member States.

Before looking in detail at the all-important Articles 3 and 3A, it may be worthwhile to dwell a little on the above paragraph, for the words used reveal a political bias which may be useful to bear in mind when doing business with public bodies or the Commission. If one is applying for an EC grant, attempting to secure a public contract, or deciding on an area of research, the above principles and aspirations should be kept in mind. Later chapters will reveal how this paragraph describes the land of opportunities and regulations represented by the single market. Note the references to respecting the environment, sustainable growth, convergence, social protection, quality of life, and economic and social cohesion, all of which will be dealt with in the chapters which follow.

First, however, Articles 3 and 3A, which state that the activities of the Community shall include:

- The elimination of customs duties and quantitative restrictions on the import and export of goods.
- A common commercial policy.
- An internal market characterized by the abolition, between member states, of obstacles to the free movement of goods, persons, services and capital.
- Measures concerning the entry and movement of persons in the internal market.
- A common policy in the sphere of agriculture and fisheries.
- A common policy on transport.
- A system ensuring that competition in the internal market is not distorted.
- The approximation of the laws of member states to the extent required for the functioning of the Common Market.
- A policy in the social sphere comprising a European Social Fund.
- The strengthening of economic and social cohesion.
- A policy in the sphere of the environment.
- The strengthening of the competitiveness of Community industry.
- The promotion of research and technological development.
- Encouragement for the establishment and development of trans-European networks.
- A contribution to the attainment of a high level of health protection.
- A contribution to education and training of quality and to the flowering of the cultures of the member states.
- A policy in the sphere of development cooperation.
- The association of the overseas countries and territories in order to increase trade and promote jointly economic and social development.
- A contribution to the strengthening of consumer protection.
- Measures in the sphere of energy, civil protection and tourism.

Article 3A emphasizes an open market economy and free competition and introduces the single currency, single monetary and exchange rate policies.

Out of the over 60,000 words in the Maastricht Treaty, Article 3 alone could serve as the basis for this book, as it contains virtually all of the opportunities, regulations and relevant elements of infrastructure appropriate to our subject.

The above list gives an indication of the range of opportunities and restrictions. On the positive side, the elimination of customs and restrictions on quantities, establishment of common business methods, the abolition of barriers to trade, the elimination of unfair competition, support to less favoured regions, science and technology grants, new information networks, ease of tendering. On the negative side, however, we see the first indications of rigid standardization in the approximation of the laws of the member states, we see the beginnings of new burdens of workers' rights, environmental, health and safety regulations, certification requirements, product liability, consumer protection, and public liability.

CHAPTER 2

Citizenship and Free Movement

The treaty states that citizenship of the union is hereby established. Every person holding the nationality of a member state shall be a citizen of the union. Citizens of the union shall enjoy the rights conferred by the treaty and shall be subject to the duties imposed thereby.

For some years now, two decades in the case of the older member states, citizens of the EC have experienced some of these benefits. Arriving at an airport of a member state, they would have been comforted by the sight of two routes through immigration: one with a sign saying 'EC Nationals' and one 'Non-EC Nationals'. Going through the former meant a cursory glance only to ensure that one was indeed a passport-holder of a member state. Now even that special channel is gone and, for EC nationals, the route is open from the aircraft – no immigration, no customs, for not only is citizenship established, but so also is free movement. Every citizen of the union shall have the right to move and reside freely within the territory of the member states.

This development marks a great moment in the history of Europe, when citizens of all of the twelve member states can travel across borders freely, as never before. Such an arrangement already existed to an extent between certain free trade areas, such as Ireland and the UK, and the Scandinavian countries, but it was a free movement of persons only, with no immigration requirements, not necessarily of goods, as customs still existed. Similar freedoms could be seen at the US–Canadian border, but, unlike the Ireland–UK borders over which anyone could cross freely, one had to be Canadian or American to have such free access on the North American border, but even in that case customs were in operation.

Later we shall see that 'customs free' does not amount to 'excise duty free', and as far as the individual's movements and activities are concerned, he or she can now move freely and act within the twelve member states with the same freedoms that exist in his or her home member state. This is not so for a citizen of a state outside the twelve, who now becomes sharply defined as a foreigner, subject to both customs and immigration at the point of entry, into any country among the twelve, and subject to passport checks at any internal frontier.

These restrictions and the lifting of them for citizens of the union are almost trivial, however, compared with the great achievement of freedom of movement and action. Take employment for example. Any citizen may take up employment anywhere in the union, subject only to local tax and social security requirements. Foreigners will still need work permits. Citizens can obtain unemployment and other social benefits on proof of residence.

However, the freedom with the greatest potential is that any citizen can travel, buy and sell, acquire property, invest, and transport products, as freely across the territories of the union as in his or her home member state. At first glance it might seem that this freedom also extends to any outsider with money, and it does to a large extent, but, as we shall see later in the chapters on public procurement, much red tape has been eliminated for the citizens of the twelve member states.

Every citizen of the union, residing in a member state of which he or she is not a national, shall have the right to vote. This has caused some controversy as it means that within national territories certain 'foreigners' can now vote. Not only may all citizens vote, but those born in other member states may also stand as candidates in municipal elections in the state where they reside, under the same conditions as nationals of the state. This is qualified in that the 'right shall be exercised subject to detailed arrangements to be adopted before 31 December 1994 by the Council, acting unanimously, on a proposal from the Commission and after consulting the European Parliament; these arrangements may provide for derogations where warranted by problems specific to a member state'.

We now move to a most interesting new right. Every citizen of the union, in the territory of a third country in which his or her home member state is not represented, shall be entitled to protection by the diplomatic or consular authorities of *any* member state, on the same conditions as the nationals of that state. Before 31 December 1993, member states shall establish the necessary rules among themselves and start the international regulations required to secure this protection.

This is, of course, as it says, for protection, but individual business people need to test this to see if it also means an expansion of business services, such as contacts and access to databases in foreign countries. This would be particularly useful to individuals from smaller member states whose governments might not have extensive representation beyond the major non-EC countries. If the spirit of the union is to be as it appears to want to be, then this may indeed mean an expansion of services to union exporters worldwide – and a lot of extra work for commercial attachés, especially those in the embassies of the larger countries.

Every citizen of the union shall have the right to petition the European Parliament and appeal to the European Ombudsman. This greatly increases the potential for complaints from aggrieved citizens who formerly had access only to national bureaux of consumer affairs and local ombudsmen.

Within the Title II section of the treaty, Article 57 states the following:

> In order to make it easier for persons to take up and pursue activities as self-employed persons, the Council shall issue directives for the mutual recognition of diplomas, certificates and other evidence of formal qualifications.

This somewhat confusing sentence appears to apply to those self-employed people whose activities are covered by regulations already in existence in member states, such as doctors or pharmacists. The section continues:

The Council shall issue directives for the consideration of the provisions laid down by law, regulation or administrative action in Member States concerning the taking up and pursuit of activities of self-employed persons. The Council, acting unanimously on a proposal from the Commission and after consulting the European Parliament, shall decide on directives, the implementation of which involves in at least one Member State amendment of the existing principles laid down by law governing the professions with respect to training and access for natural persons.

And, finally, this is added to by the following statement:

In the case of the medical and allied and pharmaceutical professions, the progressive abolition of restrictions shall be dependent upon co-ordination of the conditions for their exercise in the various Member States.

This is a very tricky area, with potential for both freeing the market and restricting it. The directives mentioned are like all EC directives produced under the administration of the Commission, but compiled by technical experts from the member states, many representing specific industries and professions. A number of forces and motivations may affect these and all other EC directives, and these include both good and bad, where the good have the general good of the profession, the general community of citizens, and the spirit of the union in mind, and where the bad seek to advance narrow sectoral or professional interests and to consolidate or create cartels or private interest groups.

While we have to live with associations of pilots, surgeons and nuclear physicists, for the sake of our health and safety, we must guard against so called 'professional qualifications' and standards being used to bolster groups of middlemen already operating closed shops. This is of particular relevance in those areas of the single market which involve the environment, quality control, auditing and consultancy, and interested parties should ensure that through national organizations they have some representations on the technical committees involved with generating directives which could affect their business, and, in particular, to ensure that a competitive and open market is not eroded by the enhancement of closed shops. The most fundamental requirement of any industry or professional group is to know what is going on at Commission level with regard to the creation of directives – packaging directives, for example, could affect a large number of sectors, while environmental directives affect us all.

This book is aimed at companies doing business in the internal market, but the freedom of movement of individual workers may also be important to readers. Throughout 1993, the European Centre for Development of Vocational Training (CEDEFOP) was involved in a process of harmonizing qualifications, that is establishing comparisons between training qualifications within the EC. It was expected that by the end of 1993 qualifications in each member state would have comparable equivalents in the other member states. Local employment services offices make this information available and they are able to give:

- The name of the corresponding qualification in each member state.
- The appropriate job title and job description.
- The tasks involved in the activities relating to the occupation.

To help one find employment, there is The European Employment Services Agency (EURES), which provides information about employment opportunities within the EC. Its purpose is to assist the free movement of workers, and it also offers the unemployed access to a wide range of job opportunities, whether unskilled, skilled, or professional.

Job vacancies in member states may be advertised in employment services agencies in other member states. These agencies advise that job seekers interested in working in another member state should not accept a job offer without having first received a formal written contract of employment which should state information relating to conditions of work including hours and salary. There is a job placement service within these agencies called The European Placement Service (SEDOC).

When travelling to negotiate for, or take up, employment, one should carry a birth certificate, a Form EI 11 from the local health board, which entitles one to health cover in any EC country, a marriage certificate if married, a typed *curriculum vitae*, copies of educational certificates, driving licence if applicable, references, Social Welfare Entitlement sheets which list entitlements available, should one need assistance and a passport.

The unemployed may transfer unemployment benefit to another member state for up to three months before taking up benefits in that member state. The same social advantages, employment and state training services apply in all member states.

For employers in Ireland, Greece, Spain and Portugal there are a number of employment incentive subsidy schemes. These are to encourage employers to take on extra workers. There is one serious limitation from the potential employer's point of view – those employed must have been unemployed for some time prior to taking up the subsidized employment.

Most member states also operate job training schemes which subsidize new workers while on job training. The snag here also is that the trainee must previously have been unemployed. There are also social employment schemes for disadvantaged groups.

The EC Petra programme operates training projects, transnational partnerships, job placements and finance schemes for cooperatives formed by youth and disadvantaged groups throughout the Community. Two groups in particular are favoured: these are women and disadvantaged groups. There are also schemes known as Youth Initiative Programmes. Petra is a no fuss programme with very little red tape. The grant is large in proportion to what needs to be earned – 70 per cent is common and some 100 per cent grants are available.

Particularly attractive to the Petra programme are groups of disadvantaged young women, physically handicapped for example. Such a group making an approach with an idea, for a working cooperative for example, should have a high chance of success.

There are few business opportunities for companies or consultants with these groups, as one would have to offer one's services or advice on a voluntary basis, but they are very interesting, particularly for people developing ideas in training, and they could have good public relations implications for local companies who get involved. They are also very worthwhile and can be rewarding in unexpected ways. Free movement extends also to capital about which the treaty has this to say:

> All restrictions on the movement of capital between Member States and between Member States and third countries shall be prohibited. All restrictions on payments between Member States and between Member States and third countries shall be prohibited.

It goes on to recognize that after 31 December 1993, by which time, the provisions should be in force, third countries may still be applying restrictions in respect to capital moving to or from them and involving such investments as real estate, securities and so on.

However, on this subject the Treaty suggests that if third countries do restrict the movement of capital to or from the union, the Council may, acting by a qualified majority on a proposal from the Commission, adopt measures on the movement of capital to or from third countries involving direct investment, including investment in real estate or the admission of securities to capital markets, or the provision of financial services. And in an interesting addition, it says that unanimity shall be required for measures under this paragraph 'which constitute a step back in Community law as regards the liberalization of the movement of capital to or from third countries'. So for businesses from such third countries, this would appear to be warning of pressure that can be applied.

Finally, in the case of the movement of capital, if any member states still enjoy a derogation allowing them to restrict movement, by 31 December 1995, at the latest, all such restrictions must be removed.

In addition, to the great single market, and union, as described above in which all citizens have free movement, these citizens have one further right, which extends to a group of third countries. The European Community also has an agreement, signed in 1991, to operate, from 1 January 1993, a 19-nation European Economic Area (EEA) with the seven European Free Trade Association (EFTA) countries. These are Austria, Finland, Iceland, Norway, Sweden, Switzerland and Lichtenstein.

The EC will maintain its border controls on the frontiers with EFTA countries, but the following freedoms exist for EC citizens. Apart from the operation of some restrictions by Switzerland and Lichtenstein to keep out low-paid Portuguese and Spanish workers, EC citizens may live and work in the seven EFTA countries. EFTA now implements EC directives and regulations, so that the standards which apply within the single market also apply to EFTA.

The agreement with EFTA brings in another 32 million people to the Community's 340 million, and these include the citizens of some very powerful economies. EC and EFTA exports to each other are almost equal, between £75 and £80 billion each year.

To summarize, the freedom of movement which makes the single market a reality has been achieved by the elimination or reduction of three kinds of barrier: physical, fiscal and technical. The physical were the actual barriers at frontiers imposed to ensure compliance with national customs rules and to enforce national laws prohibiting the smuggling of contraband. The fiscal barriers, which also involved the frontier controls, arose because of different systems of value added tax

(VAT), and excise duties. The technical barriers came in the form of national standards for products, quality assessments, health, safety and environmental regulations, and consumer protection. In the chapters on tighter regulations these standards will be looked at in detail.

CHAPTER 3

Uniformity of Law

This chapter, which is about a most difficult subject is divided into two sections. The first deals with the distinction between Community powers, shared powers and national powers, at the heart of which is the principle of subsidiarity, while the second simply lists what appear to be the main legal consequences and considerations for anyone doing business in the internal market. All the main elements are also covered in much more detail in later chapters. The reason for this approach is that the concept of subsidiarity is extremely difficult to understand and explain in lay terms, that is, outside the courtroom. It is hoped that the reader will not need to go beyond the main legal considerations for trading which are given in the second section of this chapter, but should that be necessary or should a more thorough understanding of subsidiarity be required, then a lawyer or a legal text ought to be consulted.

What now follows is taken from the text of a Commission document entitled *The Principle of Subsidiarity – Communication of the Commission to the Council and the European Parliament*, dated 27 October 1992, Brussels.

The document begins with an exploration of the subsidiarity principle, which translated into English appears to be saying that the Commission will not 'wield power' in those local cases where local powers are sufficient. This ensures that decisions are taken at the level closest to the ordinary citizen and that action taken by the upper echelons of the body politic should be limited.

The third paragraph is quite specific.

> In the Community context, subsidiarity means that the functions handed over to the Community are those which the Member States, at the various levels of decision-making, can no longer discharge satisfactorily.

Some may look upon this with a rather jaundiced eye, as they may feel that the EC has imposed a large amount of central legislation and intends to impose much more. Note, for example, the health and safety regulations mentioned in the second section of this chapter, the emerging environmental regulations, and the considerable body of worker protection, consumer rights and product liability legislation. The generosity of this paragraph is also balanced by the statement: 'The Member States, for their part, are required to facilitate the attainment of the Community's objectives . . .'.

Subsidiarity is a dynamic concept in the Community system, the document goes on. Far from putting Community action in a straight-jacket, it allows it to be expanded where circumstances so require and, conversely, to be restricted or abandoned where it is no longer justified. For more than forty years, the subsidiarity principle has satisfied two requirements: the need for Community action and the need to ensure that the means employed are commensurate with the objectives pursued, in other words, proportionality. This appears to qualify subsidiarity further with proportionality itself also qualified in the sense of 'intensity of action' or 'intensity of implementation', as in setting a framework directive and then using an intensive approach by spelling it out chapter and verse in detailed directives.

The document continues by saying that all the major objectives taken by the Commission have been based on a justification of the need for action.

The common policies provided for in the Treaty of Rome, the creation of a frontier-free area and the flanking policies provided for in the Single Act – all these initiatives have been fully justified by the imperatives of European integration. Everyone accepts that these tasks could only be effectively taken at European level. The results speak for themselves.

No doubt about this. The internal market, and the Union itself, could not have taken place without sweeping central action.

It then goes on to list the disappointments that certain obligations have not yet been met, such as a common transport policy and certain aspects of commercial policy. It agrees that the intensity of Community action is sometimes considerable, 'the finger being pointed in particular at excessively detailed rules in highly sensitive areas (environment, health) regarded, rightly or wrongly, as being essential to the creation of a single market.'

The subsidiarity principle is meant to regulate the exercise of powers rather than the conferment of powers. The treaty itself, which is the constitution, confers powers. A first consequence of the subsidiarity principle is that national powers are the rule and the Community's the exception. One cannot, therefore, list the powers reserved to the member states. If, however, these local powers are lacking, because of the absence of legislation, one is open to EC legislation being drawn into local courts.

The Community must demonstrate the need for action where its action is in preference to that of member states, but this will only be in areas outside the Community's 'areas of exclusive competence'.

As far as the Community's exclusive powers are concerned, these appear to embrace at least the following:

- The removal of barriers to the free movement of goods, persons, services and capital.
- The common commercial policy.
- The general rules on competition – the level playing field.
- The free organization of agricultural markets.
- Conservation of fisheries resources.
- The essential elements of transport policy.

Future areas include single monetary and exchange rate policies and the single currency, the ECU.

So the Community takes action only if and in so far as the objectives of the proposed action cannot be sufficiently achieved by the member states. Where powers are shared, measures to achieve the shared action are as follows:

- Legislative measures.
- Joint measures, as in the cohesion funds and research.
- Supportive measures – this is through, for example, support programmes.
- Complementary measures in education, culture and health.

From this it can be seen that the Community can maintain a level playing field either through making rules and regulations, or uplifting some regions with support programmes.

Under the heading of 'Subsidiarity and intensity of action', the document lists the appropriate forms of action as follows:

- Enact legislation.
  A common instrument to supplement national legislation.
  Approximation of laws.
  Harmonization (see Chapters 14 onwards on standards).
- Adopt recommendations.
- Provide financial support via regional development programmes (structural funds) or joint projects.
- Promote cooperation between member states.
- Encourage desirable forms of behaviour.
- Become a party to international agreements.

In another paragraph, it specifically points out that with the exception of legislation above, most of the options listed are based, in accordance with the principle of subsidiarity, on a partnership with those bodies which are closer to the individual than are the Community institutions, for example, regional authorities, trade associations and businesses.

The document also casts some light on the confused area of the directive and the regulation. The directive sets the required results but leaves it to the member states to choose the most effective means, such as legislation to achieve them. 'It differs from the regulation, which applies directly and in its entirety to states, firms and individuals and, where necessary, supersedes national legislation.'

It goes on:

In practice, of course, the distinction between directive and regulation has become blurred, in some areas for good reasons (need for uniform rules), but in others for less honourable ones (to avoid the detour via a national parliamentary procedure).

The paragraph then appears to dilute this by adding:

> Be that it may, the directive no longer enjoys any preference over the regulation and, when it is used, it is generally as detailed as a regulation and leaves hardly any margin of manoeuvre for transposal.

This confusion surrounds a point that is very important for anyone doing business in the EC. As will become apparent from later chapters, particularly those covering health and safety, product safety, public safety and product liability, it is the opinion of this writer that the very existence of directives, especially detailed ones, creates codes of practice that put one in a vulnerable position in the event of legal actions or claims of negligence. Any reader concerned about this should discuss it with the company lawyer or insurer. The question could be phrased as follows:

> If there is a detailed directive covering one of our products or processes and some damage occurs with one of these products or processes, is our exposure reduced by our demonstrating com- pliance with that directive?

There is no doubt in this writer's mind that this question is so important that a company policy on the matter is absolutely essential. Put at its simplest the policy should be that all company products and processes conform with EC directives, including those for which no regulation yet exists at national level.

The document finishes on this matter by saying that the directive should form a framework of general rules, the attainment of which member states have sole responsibility for. Regulations should remain the exception, to be resorted to only where there is an overriding need for uniform rules, in particular to guarantee the right and obligations of individuals and firms.

All this is, of course, still evolving and nowhere is this clearer than where the document says that there is much to be said for inserting in the legislative process a new type of instrument above the regulation, namely 'the framework law'. This would lay down the basic principles and essential rules, in keeping with the idea of a directive. It would transfer responsibility for implementing a law to the national authorities. 'National parliaments would thus acquire an active role in the Community process instead of being relegated, as all too often at present, to a rubber-stamp function for the transposal of an instrument.' It then goes on:

> On the other hand, such laws would be implemented by Community regulations in respect of those aspects which, for reasons of certainty as to the law and non-discrimination, require uniform rules.

Then there is a statement, most relevant for this writer and for unfortunate readers:

> It is not acceptable, in a Community governed by law, that individuals and firms should be forced, if they wish to know their rights in the jungle of Community legislation, to produce their own consolidated versions of the enactments in force.

And a final comment from the authors of the document:

> It is important that more decentralized procedures be introduced for supervising the application of Community law in order to avoid 'apoplexy at the centre and paralysis at the extremities'.

And to close this section before moving to practical examples of Community law for the business person, one hoped for option which the Commission was examining at the time of writing was as follows:

> In some sectors a possible system of direct application of controls by Member States themselves, with a regular series of reports to the Community institutions, leaving open the possibility of referring issues to the Court of Justice if these reports indicated an unsatisfactory situation.

We now come to the second part of this chapter – specifically for people doing business within the internal market. What is the legal position as far as doing business is concerned? Readers outside the EC will have to assume that they have a company, partner, agent, distributor or other commercial presence within the Community if this information is to apply directly to them. As a general rule, the information of relevance here to non-EC companies trading with the EC, is that their product standards and management standards, such as quality, now, and environment, shortly, must conform to European demands. Chapters 14 *et seq* deal with these specific issues. Readers in EFTA countries may read this chapter as if they were in the EC, except for any implications for full citizenship. For the practical purposes of doing business, however, everything here is valid for both EC and EFTA citizens.

The first major commercial consideration is the legal ability of any citizen in any member state to operate freely within State and Community laws anywhere in the internal market, to employ, be employed, buy, sell, move capital and goods, and so on as if he or she were in the country of their original citizenship.

The second, and most important, commercial and legal reality is that product standards have been harmonized across the EC and EFTA, through the work of CEN, the European Committee for Standardization. There is much more detail on this in later chapters, from Chapter 14 on, but the legal position is that products meeting a harmonized standard in any country of origin and tested there or elsewhere in the Community cannot again be asked to meet other national standards and to undergo repeat tests or certification.

In general the proof that one's products meet the relevant product standards, is that an acceptable harmonized quality management system is in place in the manufacturing company. The quality management standard adopted by the EC is ISO 9000 which in its EN equivalent is EN 29000 (European norm). This, interestingly, is an ISO standard with worldwide applicability, so that no country need feel excluded from European markets. See Chapter 17 for information on ISO 9000.

The regulation signalling the beginning of environmental demands is the EC Eco-audit Regulation. It is compulsory for member states to have a regulating apparatus set up from 1 January 1993 onwards, but voluntary for companies for the first four years. Just as buyers in multinational corporations (MNCs) and public procurement throughout the single market are demanding compliance to ISO 9000, this environmental regulation will increasingly become a condition for suppliers also. Details of the regulation and the only standard up to 1993 to support it, BS 7750, are given in Chapter 19.

Any reader now setting up business in the EC, or already in business, should know that the 1989 Health and Safety Regulations, which relate to employees, and compulsory since 1989, have been expanded with a number of new regulations since the beginning of 1993. These are now becoming law in each member state, but because they exist as EC directives and regulations, they have become codes of good practice, which would be dangerous to ignore as employees could bring actions for damages and even negligence against management should they be infringed.

The requirements of the health and safety regulations should be met as a matter of routine and good commercial practice, while customer demands will force both ISO 9000 and, eventually, the environmental management standard onto suppliers in Europe, but another piece of legislation is emerging and new codes of practice which will be of immense legal importance to manufacturers and distributors in the EC.

The tip of the iceberg of this legislation is product liability, and the most immediate manifestation of how it affects both manufacturers and suppliers is seen in the consumer legislation. See Chapter 16 for further details, but the implications for management go far beyond such consumer-friendly items as misleading advertising, defective products and consumer information. Under the general heading of environmental management, as described in BS 7750, we find such emerging concepts as public safety, product safety and, even, product use, in the last instance usually in the form of ergonomics, or 'usability'.

The first two are straightforward enough. A process plant, for example, has to be safe, and it behoves management to implement a control system to a standard such as BS 7750, to demonstrate responsibility. An accident involving the public in a plant in which there is no obvious formal safety management system will expose management to both corporate and personal liability. The control system is more than a legal defence: it actually safeguards against accidents. More importantly, the very existence of systems such as the EC Eco-audit Regulation, and its supporting standard, BS 7750, creates a code of good practice which becomes a legal defence, in the absence of anything else at least, in cases of accident. It also places companies who have not adopted it, or do not know about it, at a disadvantage. Because of this, we are seeing standards such as BS 7750, which began as market-led devices, becoming compliance-led, with legal and insurance motivations replacing those of public relations.

Perhaps the most interesting and complex issue of all is that of product use. If the product can endanger the users or the public, the company will be liable, and the consequences for management may also be extensive. The more ubiquitous the product and the more it is used in process-type situations, which have a potential for public safety, the greater the need to ensure that product use is covered by detailed instructions. This is best illustrated with one product, ubiquitous in its use and often in critical online situations, from flying aircraft to operating nuclear power stations. That is software.

No product better illustrates how the hierarchy of standards works, and their relationships with corporate responsibility than software. Starting at the top of the hierarchy the development of software products can be controlled by the appropriate quality management standard, ISO 9000-3, the software quality management standard. This gives assurance that a quality management standard exists to control the production of software. But software, like any other product, may have an individual standard, which is a code of good practice for its construction, and this standard is ISO 9241, a standard for both good VDU practice and software ergonomics.

The above points relate directly to software manufacturers but now a regulation exists governing the use of software, by the end user. The first part of this, already law, is the VDU Regulation, part of the health and safety regulations. An employer must ensure that employees are not damaged either by the wrong use of VDUs, or bad software, which makes VDUs difficult to use, or cause eye-strain. However, a software ergonomics code of practice has already emerged through ISO 9241. This tells software developers how to make their product 'usable' with reference to VDUs so that, for example, an operator is not confused to the point where he or she causes an accident, pressing the wrong key, resulting in an explosion or in crashing an aircraft, by switching off the wrong engine. In other words, the software messages must be clear and understandable; if not, and if they contribute to an accident, the software developers might find themselves sharing liability. But before that may happen, a new EC software ergonomics directive, based on ISO 9241, may ensure that all software users purchase only from developers who are buying products certified to ISO 9241.

Software is the extreme example, but the CE Mark, explained in some detail in Chapter 24, also demonstrates how all products covered by compulsory directives, especially those with safety considerations, now need special certification, without which they will not be purchased within the EC. For information on the CE Mark, see Chapter 24.

To summarize the legal situation for businesses selling into, or operating in, the internal market, both product certification and one's manufacturing process certified to ISO 9000 are essential requirements, while, as we move into the middle and second half of the decade, environmental regulations and standards will also become mandatory. Already many specific environmental regulations are mandatory, but what is now joining them is the need for an environment management system standard, such as BS 7750, which should shortly be embraced by an ISO equivalent.

If one is hiring staff in the EC, health and safety regulations are mandatory, and product liability requirements demand the kind of protection offered by full adherence to product standards and quality management standards.

To satisfy market demands fully, and to protect oneself legally, ensure that all products are manufactured to the appropriate standard, using the CE Mark where relevant, obtain ISO 9000 certification for each plant, together with certification to the EC-audit Regulation, using BS 7750 and the ISO equivalent when it emerges, and strictly implement the health and safety regulations for any staff member employed within the internal market. All of these requirements are covered in more detail in the chapters which follow.

Economic and Monetary Union

At the time of writing (March 1993), the prospect of monetary union, and its absence, were causing havoc to some currencies. After a sterling crisis, a number of currencies within the twelve member states were devalued. For exporters, a situation where one might find sales values cut by as much as ten per cent was almost intolerable, wiping out profitability in some cases. Monetary union is expected to introduce a single currency to all members of the union and is planned for in three stages.

During the first stage each member state had to adopt measures to free the movement of capital and to get its finances in order, particularly external debts, annual deficits and price stability. This was known as the process of convergence towards Economic and Monetary Union (EMU). The second stage which starts on 1 January 1994 is monitored by the Council and the European Commission.

A protocol at the end of the treaty lays down the provisions for the establishment of a European Monetary Institute (EMI) for the second stage. The members of the EMI are the central banks of the member states. As Luxembourg did not have a central bank for the purposes of the statute and protocol, the Institut Monetaire Luxembourgeois is regarded as a central bank. The EMI takes over the assets and liabilities of the European Monetary Co-operation Fund (EMCF), while both it and its Committee of Governors are dissolved.

The purpose of the EMI is to help create the conditions necessary for the transition to the third stage of economic and monetary union, in particular, by the following:

- Strengthening the coordination of monetary policies with a view to ensuring price stability.
- Making the preparations required for the establishment of the European System of Central Banks (ESCB), and for the conduct of a single monetary policy and the creation of a single currency in the third stage.
- Overseeing the development of the ECU.

This begins the process of making each central bank independent of its member state. At the latest by 31 December 1996, the EMI shall specify the regulatory, organizational and logistical framework necessary for the ESCB to operate in the third stage, specifically to prepare the instruments and procedures necessary for carrying out a single monetary policy, to standardize statistics, to prepare the rules for the operation of the central banks within the ESCB, to promote the efficiency of cross-border payments, and to produce the ECU bank notes. The authorities in each member state are expected to consult the EMI on any draft legislative provisions concerning it, particularly with regard to the setting up of the ESCB.

Independence is established in Article 8, which requires the EMI to act according to its own responsibilities and not to seek or take any instructions from Community institutions or bodies or governments of member states, and these also undertake to respect this principle and not to seek to influence the EMI in the performance of its tasks.

Through the Commission, the EMI will report to the Council on the progress of the member states towards monetary union. It will also report on the progress of 'convergence', which is the process of ensuring compatibility between economies in the approach to the third stage. The standards set for each state, against which they will be measured are as follows:

- An average rate of inflation not exceeding by more than 1.5 percentage points that of the three best performing states.
- A budgetary deficit less than 3 per cent of GDP, staying within the fluctuation margins of the exchange rate mechanism of the EMS without devaluation, for at least two years.
- An average nominal, long-term interest rate that does not exceed by more than two percentage points that of the three best performing states in terms of price stability.

These criteria are laid down in protocols attached to the Treaty.

All this is leading up to the adoption of a single currency at the third stage, which is planned in the following way. The EMI reports will be used to assess the performance of each member state to see if it meets the requirements for adopting the single currency. If a majority of the member states meets these requirements, the heads of government will, by the end of 1996, decide whether it is appropriate to enter the third stage. If, by the end of 1997, no date has been set for the beginning of the third stage, the third stage will begin on 1 January 1999, like it or not.

Six months before this date, and before 1 July 1998, the heads of government will confirm which member states fulfil the necessary conditions for adopting the single currency. The Council, advised by the Commission, may decide to grant a derogation to some states, who will not then participate by the following January. States with a derogation will not be able to participate in voting on decisions on EMU matters. At least once, however, in every two years the Commission can propose to abrogate the derogation of any member state if that state qualifies.

Immediately after the decision on the date for the beginning of the third stage, or, as the case may be, immediately after 1 July 1998, the following will occur.

Monetary union begins. Those governments without a derogation will appoint the president and executive board of the European Central Bank (ECB). As soon as the Executive Board is established, the tasks of the EMI will be taken over and the EMI will go into liquidation. Now comes the crunch. The third stage now begins and the Council supported by those member states without a derogation will accept a Commission proposal and, after consultation with the ECB, will adopt the conversion rates at which the currencies of the participants shall be irrevocably fixed, and at which irrevocable fixed rate the European Currency Unit (ECU) shall be substituted for these currencies, and the ECU will become a currency in its own right.

So, if we thought we had a problem deciding how to get paid for our exports before 1993, during the revaluation crises, imagine the jockeying that will go on to get investments into the best possible currency before an irrevocable rate is struck some time after 1 July 1998.

Some may even consider the US dollar or the yen as a safe temporary sanctuary. The conversion process will not be allowed to modify the external value of the ECU. If it is decided to abrogate a derogation, the Council, acting with the unanimity of the member states who are without a derogation – that is within the monetary union – and acting with the member state concerned, and also on a Commission proposal, and advised by the ECB, shall adopt a rate at which the ECU shall be substituted for the currency of the member state concerned.

From all this it will be seen that it is of great interest to companies in the EC between now and 1 July 1998 to know whether or not their state will be in the monetary union or subject to a derogation. It would seem that the first 'big bang' of being in with the monetary union group when the rates are struck is better than a later admission. What it amounts to is that the extent of one's very reserves and the value of revenues will be decided by one of these events.

The UK position

A protocol entitled 'Protocol on certain provisions relating to the United Kingdom of Great Britain and Northern Ireland' has been attached to the treaty giving the UK an opt-out position on monetary union. The UK may notify its intention to move to the third stage before 1 January 1998. It will not be obliged to do so, however, unless this is decided by its parliament; unless it decides that it will, it will be under no obligation to do so.

If it opts out, it cannot vote with other qualifying states on EMU and will not be committed to the ECB procedures or the single currency. In general it will be like other states which have not qualified. The Bank of England will continue to operate until such time as the UK may be accepted into the EMU.

Economic union

If the grand dream of a united Europe is to be fully realized it will be brought about finally by economic union, that is all member states planning for and controlling the general economy of the union. The treaty states that the member states shall conduct their economic policies with a view to contributing to the achievement of the objectives of the Community and that they shall act in accordance with the principles of an open market economy with free competition, favouring an efficient allocation of resources. It goes on to make this more specific, saying that the states shall regard their economic policies as a matter of common concern and shall coordinate them with the Council.

The Council will thus formulate economic policy, guided, of course, by the Commission, but it will go much further, monitoring it also and intervening if necessary. It could act unanimously on a proposal from the Commission to take measures in the case of severe difficulties in securing the supply of certain products, or it could grant financial assistance in the case of natural disasters.

Member states are no longer allowed to run up excessive deficits, and the Commission will monitor them in this regard. The reference values not to be exceeded are in a protocol attached to the treaty. Pressure and control will be exercised either by withholding credit through the European Investment Bank or through fines.

PART II

The Opportunities

CHAPTER 5

The Public Procurement Market

When the Single European Act was ratified at the beginning of 1987, it envisaged the completion of a single market of some 342 million consumers by the end of 1992. Most of the directives and the changes they will help bring about are familiar to us, such as those affecting the movement of products, capital and people, but a huge and, up to now, almost separate area is that of public procurement within the national states of the Community members. The opening up of public procurement has for a long time being recognized as a fundamental component of the real single market, emerging at the beginning of 1993.

At its simplest, public procurement is purchasing by state authorities, central governments, local agencies and state enterprises. Before these moves, a very small percentage, as low as 2 per cent according to some commentators, was bought outside national boundaries. The European Commission has vigorously pursued the objective of opening up this market with a number of directives. It now believes that both the political framework and legal decision making apparatus exist to achieve this.

France is regarded as a model for Europe and was an inspiration to the EC in drawing up the public procurement directives, and we find that *Le Code Des Marchés Public Français* already complies with most of these directives. It is useful therefore to look at France and ask what are the public procurement bodies in that country.

They are first the central state bodies, including those administered directly by them, such as universities and national cultural institutions; then, the regional bodies in 26 regions, 100 departments, 36,527 communities, and other specific regional institutions, such as hospitals; then, 170 national enterprises, controlled by the state. The best known are SNCF, Air France, EDF (electricity), and GDF (Gas).

In 1985 the Commission reviewed its progress towards creating a single market and decided in a published white paper that it still had a long way to go before a genuine common market could exist. A crash programme began to remove the remaining barriers and to create a real single market of over 340 million people in 12 countries by the end of 1992. Over 300 pieces of legislation have been involved in the attempt to complete the single market. The partitioning of national markets also inhibited many European companies from achieving the economies of scale needed to compete with the US and Japan. The sheer size alone of public purchasing made it a prime target for the EC planners.

What the Community has tried to do is to make the rules of competing for public business as clear as possible, eliminate red tape and encourage those who feel excluded to complain if the public buyers appear to be breaking the rules.

The value of public procurement is £455 billion or 15 per cent of total Community GDP. This is greater than the amount the twelve member states currently spend trading with each other, so the impact of it being available across frontiers is potentially enormous. For example, the UK spends 21 per cent of GDP on public procurement, most of it at home.

Ninety per cent of all manufactured telecommunications equipment, and of measuring and electromedical equipment goes to public procurement, that is, it is bought by the state. Fifty per cent of aircraft and aviation sales are to the state, and 60 per cent of all office and data processing equipment.

Despite these substantial figures, only 2 per cent of all buying was, prior to these new measures, bought across borders from other EC states. The EC estimates that this has wasted £15 billion of taxpayers money each year, apart from being against the spirit of the single market.

In the 1985 review of progress, the Commission found that the earlier directives and their expectations were not being realised. Purchasing entities and public authorities undertaking construction projects, for example, were continuing to give preference to domestic suppliers and contractors. The so called 'excluded sectors' of the public utilities were also proving to be major loopholes. The recessions of the 1970s after the first oil crisis had not helped either. Chiefly, however, the early legislation had not brought about the needed transparency in tendering and award procedures, so that there was often no way of detecting, let alone preventing, discrimination against non-national prospective suppliers. The main violations were:

- Failure to advertise in the *Official Journal of the European Communities*.
- Single tendering.
- Discrimination in the use of red tape, especially insistence on compliance with national standards.
- Discriminatory selection criteria.

A note of warning, however. Side by side with the changes being realized through both legislation and the new European spirit are existing developments in the global marketplace. One of these is the changing relationship between buyer and supplier and this is so important that it is dealt with in Chapter 11, selling to the multi-national corporations (MNCs). In essence what is happening is that large buyers, particularly those operating to so called 'world-class' standards are dealing with fewer suppliers and doing so in closer relationships. This is particularly true where there are demands for operating in a paperless trading environment, such as with electronic data interchange (EDI) and in just-in-time delivery (JIT). In these cases, the demands of the operational environment may dictate the number of suppliers, for example, it could be difficult to practise open procurement if every new supplier had to communicate via an established EDI system or a demanding JIT mode, such as delivering with zero defects to point of use, with hospital supplies for instance.

The effects of protection have been described as the 'shot in the arm which becomes a shot in the foot'. European industry has been weak due, to some extent, to dependence on national markets which are too small for optimum performance. This has been very true in the high technology sectors, and nowhere more apparent than with computers, aerospace and telecommunications.

The high-tech industries are usually very dependent on state buying and generally also state-operated. This has a negative effect on competition and on subsequent research, development and innovation. It is now believed that an open public procurement market will greatly enhance the possibilities of European companies coming up with new, commercially exploitable products.

Most of the legislation dealing with the procurement of public works and supplies has been in place since 1990 for nine member states. Greece, Spain and Portugal were allowed, until March 1992, to implement all the legislation in these two areas. In cases where some national governments were allowed to use the award of contracts as a form of aid to companies in areas being helped through regional development programmes, these practices were allowed to continue up to January 1993.

Finally, the Single European Act itself, which came into force in 1987, established measures such as majority voting, which ensured that all the directives and their amendments would be in place by 1993, including any other mechanisms needed to maintain a real single market. One of its most important aims was to create a single European market. To this end it set a firm date of midnight 31 December 1992 for the elimination of most of the remaining internal barriers, and July 1993 for the open procurement of public services.

The Act stresses the importance of public procurement, claiming that it will strengthen the scientific and technological base of European industry. It also promises Community support for the efforts of companies to cooperate with each other to exploit the potential of the internal market, in particular in the business of national public contracts, and in the establishment of common standards and the removal of barriers in doing so.

The actual public procurement measures

In the 1985 review it became apparent that it was vital to open up the public procurement markets for both the good of European industry and for the EC economy itself, and that the current legislation needed amendment. By March 1987, a reform package was underway. The reforms were aimed at applying the three free trade principles, on which the original concept of the common market was based, to the public sector's purchases of goods and services.

The first of these principles is the prohibition of measures which restrict trade between member states. This includes not only direct restrictions on imports but also regulations or requirements (such as standards or tendering procedures) that indirectly have the same effect as import restrictions.

The second principle is that companies and individuals from any member state should be free to set up in business in any other member state. This freedom means that no special or more onerous requirements may be placed on an EC 'foreign' business resident within the member state.

The third principle is that no restrictions may be placed on non-resident businesses providing services in other member states, a vitally important principle as will be seen when we look later at the potential of the services market.

The Commission's reform package called for action on four fronts.

1. To make tendering and award procedures more transparent, by overhauling the existing legislation.
2. To introduce rules for EC-wide competitive tendering for those sectors excluded from the original legislation.
3. To open up the procurement of services.
4. To tighten up enforcement measures.

All of these reforms also took the interests of small and medium-sized companies into account to ensure that they also received a fair share of the business, so that it would not all go to the larger companies.

The reforms can be summarized as follows:

- The amendments of the existing directives on public works and supplies contracts.
- The introduction of new directives on services, on the so called excluded sectors, and on remedies.
- The creation of an EC-wide market information system, including the daily publication of business of a certain value, and the creation of an online tendering system called the Tenders Electronic Daily (TED) database.

The public procurement elements

The main elements of public procurement from the point of view of prospective suppliers are:

- Public works, such as buildings and roads.
- Public supply. This is virtually everything bought by public buyers, in the form of goods.
- The so-called excluded sectors of telecommunications, energy, drinking water supply and transport.
- Services.

The directives have also greatly improved the review procedures allowing for complaints and penalties.

The directives removed previous ambiguities stating that procurement was not just outright purchase, but also leasing, rental or hire purchase. Buyers had been cheating on the contract value threshold of ECU 200,000 set by the 1977 legislation which stated that all of the rules about public procurement related to contracts above the threshold for supplies and to above ECU 1,000,000 for works. Methods of splitting and undervaluing contracts had evolved to by-pass the legislation. The new legislation prohibited splitting. The 1989 Amendment to the Works Directive increased the threshold for works contracts to ECU 5,000,000, but demanded that certain split lots of ECU 1,000,000 be included.

EC-wide tendering and its advertising are demanded. This is done in hard copy through the daily published *Official Journal Supplement* and TED, its electronic version, Tenders Electronic Daily.

An important new requirement is that buyers of supplies exceeding ECU 750,000 have to give more than six months notice in 'advanced notices' published in the *Official Journal*. Up to now most announcements of tenders have given only between four and six weeks notice. A good tip, however, is to look at these one year in advance as many are annual, especially for supplies, and one can deduce what will be repeated by the nature of the supplies sought, for example stationery or other consumables.

Another new requirement for buyers is to publish a notice on the outcome of each tender in the *Official Journal Supplement*, which ensures that business is done as openly as possible.

New rules on tendering

There are two general kinds of tenders: open and restricted. There is also a category of negotiated tenders for certain specific cases. The rules now are that selective or restricted tenders are allowed only in certain justifiable cases, for example in highly specific product cases. Those using restricted tenders have both to justify them and report on them. Open tendering has now become the rule.

In the case of open tenders, the closing date is now not less than 52 days from dispatch of the tender notice for publication in the *Official Journal*.

Under the new legislation, it is now obligatory to refer only to EC standards, such as the EN numbered series, when specifying standards in calls for tenders. National standards may, of course, be specified where they also implement an EC standard. What this means in this case is that the national standard, such as a BS, has an equivalent EC standard. Where a quality management system is demanded, which is in most cases for manufacturers, this will be ISO 9000, under the title of its EN equivalent, EN 29000.

Where the European standards are absent, readers should check with their national standards authority, but the rather complex EC ruling is that in the absence of European standards or common technical specifications, purchasers may refer, subject to the principles of equivalence and mutual recognition of national technical specifications, to other documents. The ruling continues:

> In that case they are recommended to refer (in order) to national standards implementing international standards and to other national standards.

This is very difficult to interpret, but it helps if we look at the cases where purchasers may depart from the rules 'in certain specified circumstances', but where they must justify doing so. These cases are where:

- The standards do not include provision for establishing conformity or no satisfactory technical means of establishing conformity exists.
- Application of the rule would run counter to Community provisions for telecommunications.
- It would oblige the purchaser to accept products incompatible with equipment already in use or would entail disproportionate costs or disproportionate technical difficulties.
- The project is genuinely innovative, making reference to existing standards inappropriate.

This rather complex set of rules on exceptions makes more sense when we realize that some countries have many more or better product standards than others, and that the process of harmonizing national standards is still going on, as is the process of establishing the European EN standards. Too heavy a reliance on standards could also stifle innovation, as new products and processes cannot wait for standards to emerge first.

Public works

In general this term refers to construction, demolition, civil engineering, installation and decoration. The directives apply to public works contracts, and these are defined as contracts for pecuniary consideration concluded in writing between a contractor and an authority awarding contracts and concerning activities in the construction sector. The contractor may be a company, an individual or consortia.

The threshold beyond which the rules apply is ECU 5,000,000 before VAT and ECU 1,000,000 in the case of certain split lots. The rules specify the advertising of contracts, the tendering procedures, closing dates, the different kinds of tenders, the disqualification and elimination of contractors, the criteria to be used in awarding contracts, the rules for sub-contracting, and complaint procedures.

Public supplies

Public supplies cover a huge range of possibilities from toilet paper to bus shelters. The threshold beyond which the rules apply is ECU 200,000 before VAT. There is a different threshold, usually lower and currently around ECU 130,000 for certain government agencies who cooperate under the GATT Government Procurement Code. These are usually central government departments and the bodies whose purchasing they control.

Public supply contracts are defined as contracts for pecuniary consideration concluded in writing between a supplier and a co-contracting authority, or purchaser, for the supply of products. The contract may, in addition, cover siting and installation work, which presumably means that a contract can be for both supply and works. As with public works, the supplier may be a company, individual or consortia. Undervaluation by splitting a purchase is prohibited.

The rules lay down conditions for advertising, sources of information, tendering procedures, closing dates, the disqualification or elimination of contractors and the criteria used in awarding contracts.

The so-called excluded sectors

The reason for adding 'so-called' to the title of the excluded sectors is that most of the Commission's recent activities in this area have been to exert pressure to open up these sectors, so that the emphasis nowadays is more on how they are being opened up, rather than a reiteration of the facts of their exclusion.

The excluded sectors can be regarded as public utilities dealing in the four large areas of telecommunications, energy, drinking water supply and transport. This is not as simple as it looks. The exclusions, for example, have applied only to supplies in telecommunications, not works or services, and do not apply to airport authorities or irrigation services.

The one other major exclusion area is arms and other military material, but there are even Community pressures to open up defence purchasing.

Services

This was covered in one of the last public procurement directives in 1993, and was a dramatic new element in the opening up of public procurement for the internal market. The purchases of services are considerable both in size and in their potential for suppliers of all sizes. They account for no less than 20 per cent of total public sector purchasing, and apply to all public bodies, central, regional, local, state enterprises, and public authorities.

A public service contract is a contract for pecuniary interest concluded in writing between a supplier and a contracting authority. While it covers a huge range of services, from PR to architecture, it excludes arbitration and conciliation services, acquisition of programming material by broadcasters, contracts for the purchase, lease or rental of, or concerning rights on land, existing buildings or other immovable property, contracts concerning primary issues of government bonds and other activities in the area of public debt management, and, finally, public service concessions.

The thresholds beyond which the rules apply are ECU 200,000 plus VAT, and ECU 100,000 for annual insurance premiums. Certain architectural and engineering services which involve the complete design of work worth ECU 5,000,000 plus VAT also come within the rules. The rules lay down the types of tender procedure, advertising, selection, award of contracts, and the provision of information.

The review procedures

So important is review to ensure the workings of the open market in public procurement that a separate review directive was adopted in 1989. It appeared that original directives were inadequate in matters of redress where a contractor had been discriminated against. The review directive sets out the steps which can be taken by such a tenderer and the powers and provisions of the Commission in taking corrective action or imposing penalties.

CHAPTER 6

Public Works

The aims of the public works directives are to open up the public construction markets of the EC through EC-wide competitive tendering and to ensure that tendering procedures are open and above board. It will be noticed that although there are different directives for works and supplies, referred to sometimes as construction and procurement, many of the rules are similar, particularly concerning advertising, the prohibition of discriminatory specifications, and the use of objective criteria for disqualifying or eliminating contestants.

The directives apply to public works contracts, defined as contracts for financial consideration in writing between a contractor and an authority awarding contracts for activities in the construction sectors. Terms of the contract are not included, so that how one is paid is not of interest to the legislators.

Contractors may be companies, firms, individuals or consortia. Consortia are not obliged to assume any particular legal form to bid for a contract, but may be required to do so if the contract is awarded to them.

The activities falling within the public works definition are described in the following list, taken from the EC's standard industrial classification, called NACE.

Group 500

500 Building and civil engineering

General building and civil engineering work (without any particular specialization) and demolition work.

    500.1 General building and civil engineering work (without any particular specialization).
    500.2 Demolition work.

501 Construction of flats, office blocks, hospitals and other buildings, both residential and non-residential

    501.1 General building contractors.
    501.2 Roofing.
    501.3 Construction of chimneys, kilns and furnaces.
    501.4 Waterproofing and damp proofing.
    501.5 Restoration and maintenance of outside walls (repointing, cleaning, etc.).
    501.6 Erection and dismantlement of scaffolding.
    501.7 Other specialized activities relating to construction work (including carpentry).

502 Civil engineering: construction of roads, bridges, railways etc.

    502.1 General civil engineering work.
    502.2 Earth moving (navvying).
    502.3 Construction of bridges, tunnels and shafts, drilling.

502.4 Hydraulic engineering (rivers, canals, harbours, flows, locks and dams).

502.5 Road-building (including specialized construction of airports and runways.

502.6 Specialized construction work relating to water (i.e. to irrigation, land drainage, water supply, sewage disposal, sewerage, etc.).

502.7 Specialized activities in other areas of civil engineering.

503 Installation (fittings and fixtures)

503.1 General installation work.

503.2 Gas fitting and plumbing, and the installation of sanitary equipment.

503.3 Installation of heating and ventilation apparatus (central heating, air conditioning, ventilation).

503.4 Sound and heat insulation, insulation against vibration.

503.5 Electrical fitting.

503.6 Installation of aerials, lighting conductors, telephones etc.

504 Building completion work

504.1 General building completion work.

504.2 Plastering.

504.3 Joinery, primarily engaged in on the site assembly and/or installation (including the laying of parquet flooring).

504.4 Painting, glazing, paper-hanging.

504.5 Tiling and otherwise covering floors and walls.

504.6 Other building completion work (putting in fireplaces, etc.).

The authorities subject to the legislation

The authorities whose construction contracts are subject to the legislation are the state, that is, central government agencies, regional or local authorities, and other 'legal persons governed by public law' or equivalent bodies.

Across the twelve member states this would include such diverse organizations as association de communes, syndicates de communes, Gemeindeverbande, public assistance commissions, Church structures (Belgium), state universities and institutes, some relief and charity organizations (Italy), the Dutch TNO, the Scottish Special Housing Association and the Northern Ireland Housing Executive.

The contracts covered are all those worth ECU 5,000,000 before VAT. This threshold figure is converted into national currencies at the fixed exchange rate each year for the following year and published every November in the *Official Journal*, for example, £3,500,000 for the UK, or whatever, depending on any year's exchange rate. Contracts of £1,000,000 may also be affected as will be seen from the following paragraphs.

The directive is very explicit about the rules. The value must include the value of the work contracted for, as well as the cost of the supplies needed to carry out the work, even if these are provided to the contractor by the principal. It is prohibited to split up contracts in order to take them below the threshold.

When a work is divided into several lots, each one the subject of a contract, the value of each lot must be included in an aggregate value of the lots and if this exceeds the threshold then the provisions of the directive apply to all the lots.

The authorities can depart from the provisions for lots whose estimated value before VAT is less than ECU 1,000,000, provided that the total estimated value of all the exempted lots does not exceed 20 per cent of the total value of the project. So lots of ECU 1,000,000 may well come within the provisions.

Key requirements of the directive are EC-wide competitive tendering and compulsory advertising of contracts in the *Official Journal Supplement*. There is a prescribed format for the layout and contents of the tender notice. Notices must be concise, staying within a maximum length of one page of 650 words of the Journal. There are two models, one for open and one for restricted or selective tenders.

The technical specifications

One of the strengths of the directives is the plugging of loopholes allowing the use of local specifications as technical barriers to competition. The directive demands the use of those national standards which also represent or implement European standards, or reference to

European technical approvals, such as certification schemes. Readers should use the information services of their national standards authorities, as many different standards schemes are now harmonized within the EC, and are represented nationally by bodies such as the BSI in the UK.

Authorities are allowed to depart from the provisions in the following cases.

- Where there is no method, as yet, for establishing conformity to the standards – viz. no certification scheme or agency capable of certification.
- Where the use of the standards or specifications would make existing equipment obsolete or entail disproportionate costs or technical difficulties.
- Where the project is of a genuinely innovative nature.
- It is also prohibited to specify particular products, processes or sources, which would either favour or eliminate individual companies. The indication of trade marks, patents, types or the specific origin or type of production are prohibited. Where the authorities awarding the contract are unable to give a description sufficiently precise and intelligible they may indicate one of the above (trade marks or equivalent) with the words 'or equivalent'.

Tendering procedures

There are three kinds of tendering procedures: open, restricted and negotiated.

Open tendering speaks for itself, restricted tendering is where only contractors invited by the contracting authority submit tenders, while negotiated tendering is where the contracting authorities consult contractors of their choice and negotiate with one or more of them. The difference between open and restricted, is that in the latter case a selection is made from the contractors who reply to the tender notice and the selected contractors only are invited to bid.

In the case of negotiated procedures the contracting authorities select contractors of their choice and negotiate terms of contract with one or more of them. The negotiated procedure is allowed in the following cases, after prior publication and the selection according to the normal criteria:

- In the event of irregular tenders in response to an open or restricted procedure.
- When the works involved are carried out purely for the purpose of research, experiment or development.
- In exceptional cases where the nature of the works or the risks attaching to them do not allow full estimation of costs.

Furthermore, the contracting authority can in some specified cases award a public works contract by negotiated procedure without prior publication of a tender notice. These cases are:

- In the absence of tenders in response to an open or restricted procedure.
- When for technical or artistic reasons or for reasons connected with the protection of exclusion rights, the works may only be carried out by a particular contractor.
- When, because of unforeseen events, there is extreme urgency and the prescribed time limits cannot be met.
- Where the new works are a repetition of similar works carried out by the same contractors.

To further reduce the opportunities of abuse by using negotiated procedures, the following measures are also required.

Within 15 days of a request for information about rejection for a rejected candidate, the contracting authority must respond with the reasons for rejection and the name of the successful tenderer. The reasons must also be sent to the Office for Official Publications of the EC. Finally, the contracting authority has to draw up a written report which must be available on request to the Commission for each contract awarded under negotiated procedures.

In the rules for selection of contractors which follow, it will be seen that in the case of restrictive procedures, at least five contractors must be involved in invitations to tender, and up to twenty may be involved. In the case of negotiated procedures there must be not less than three unless there is an insufficient number to provide three. This is to ensure genuine competition in both cases.

The effect of all these conditions for negotiated contracts, plus the openness of the advertising for both open and restricted tenders, makes it difficult for contracting authorities to abuse the system. Two other factors must be considered: first, most if not all of the contracting authorities are in turn open to both managerial and public scrutiny, which encourages them to make economically correct decisions; and second, the spirit of the single market, if not the directives, encourages buyers to be fair and honest.

The real proof, however, is in the number of invitations for open tenders appearing daily in the *Official Journal*, which suggests that the open public procurement market has become a reality.

Time limits for tenders

The time limits for the receipt of tenders are:

- For open procedures not less than 52 days from the date of dispatch of the notice to the *Official Journal*. Where an advance notice has been published, the time limit for the receipt of tenders may be reduced to 36 days.
- Six days after receiving requests for contract and supporting documents these must be sent by the contracting authorities.
- In the case of restricted and negotiated procedures, the time limit for receipt of requests to participate shall be not less than 37 days from the date of dispatch of the notice.
- In the case of restricted procedures, the time limit for receipt of tenders may not be less than 40 days from the date of dispatch of the written invitations. This may be reduced to 36 days where advanced notice has been published.

The rules for selection

The directives have made these quite specific. The rules fall into two categories – *who* can participate and *how* the award is made. First, let us deal with participation. The directives provide for the following:

- Where the criterion for the award of the contract is that of the most economically advantageous tender, contracting authorities may take account of variances which are submitted by a tenderer and meet the minimum specifications required by the contracting authority.

- In the contract document, the contracting authority may ask the tenderer to indicate in his tender any share of the contract he may intend to subcontract to third parties.
- Where the contracting authorities award a contract by restrictive procedure, they may prescribe the range within which the number of undertakings which they intend to invite will fall. In this case the range shall be indicated in the contract notice. The range will be determined in the light of the work to be carried out. The range must number at least 5 undertakings and may be up to 20. In any event, the number of candidates invited to tender shall be sufficient to ensure genuine competition.
- Where the contracting authorities award a contract by negotiated procedure, the number of candidates admitted to negotiate may not be less than 3 provided that there is a sufficient number of suitable candidates.

Having got these rather legal criteria out of the way, the main considerations for whether or not one can participate can be listed as follows:

- Financial soundness and standing.
- Technical competence.
- General standing.

Purchasers are entitled to check the financial soundness and technical competence of bidders before selecting them to bid or considering their bids, and to eliminate those who fail to qualify. As evidence of technical capability the promoters may require to see the professional qualifications of the contractor, a list of the construction work carried out over the previous 5 years, particulars of plant and equipment, labour and staff resources, and the technical resources that may be called upon. Accounts and bank statements can be admitted as financial evidence.

On the general standing side, the author hopes that none of the following apply to readers, as some of them relate to the possibility of grave professional misconduct. The following lists grounds on which any supplier may be disqualified.

1. A supplier who is bankrupt or, being wound up, has ceased or suspended trading, or is operating under court protection pending a settlement with creditors, or is in any analogous situation arising from national proceedings of a similar nature.

2. A supplier who is the subject of proceedings for bankruptcy, winding-up or court protection pending a settlement with creditors, or national proceedings of a similar nature.

3. A supplier who has been convicted of an offence concerning his professional conduct by a judgement which has the force of *res judicata*.

4. A supplier who can be shown by the contracting authority to have been guilty of grave professional misconduct.

5. A supplier who has not fulfilled obligations relating to payment of social security contributions under the statutory provision of his country of residence or of the country of the contracting authority.

6. A supplier who has not fulfilled obligations relating to payment of taxes under the statutory provisions of his country of residence or the country of the contracting authority.

7. A supplier who has been guilty of serious misrepresentation in supplying information about his current standing or past record or his financial or technical capacity.

In the cases where it is up to the supplier to show that he is not in any of the stated situations (i.e. all except cases (4) and (7), the procurement authority is bound to accept as satisfactory evidence:

(a) for cases (1), (2) and (3), the judicial record on the supplier or an equivalent document issued by a judicial or administrative authority in the supplier's country of origin or residence showing that none of these cases applies.

(b) for cases (5) and (6) a certificate issued by the competent authority in the member state concerned.

If such documents or certificates are not issued by the country in question or if they do not cover all the cases referred to in 1, 2 and 3, the supplier may instead produce an affidavit sworn before a judicial or administrative authority, notary or any other competent authority in the member state concerned. Instead of an affidavit, a solemn declaration may be provided. Affidavits and solemn declarations must be authenticated by the competent authority or a notary.

Finally, even the most professional bidder can be rejected if the tenders appear to be abnormally low in relation to the transaction. Up to the end of 1992 authorities could simply reject these if the numbers of tenders in question were large, but from 1992 onwards they have had to request explanations. Also, up to the end of 1992, certain national schemes involved with regional development and job creation, where contracts were given as a form of aid, had exceptions in this area.

After all of these participation questions have been answered, the awarding criteria apply. These are simply:

- Either the lowest price only, or
- when the award is made to the most economically advantageous tender, using such criteria as running costs, technical merit, delivery, cost effectiveness.

These should, however, be made clear in the contract documents and tender notice.

CHAPTER 7

Public Supplies

The main directives in public supply are the 1971 77/62 EEC directive for public supplies and the 1988 amendment 88/295/EEC, which became law for all member states on 1 March 1992.

Public Supply contracts are defined as contracts for pecuniary consideration concluded in writing between a supplier and a contracting authority (purchasing or procurement agency) for the supply of products. The contract may, in addition, cover siting and installation work (relating to the products). Suppliers may be companies, firms, individuals or consortia of such elements. The contracting bodies are the same as those referred to in the last chapter on public works, that is all state and state-owned purchasers. The amending directive makes it clear that supplies are not limited to outright purchase but extend also to leasing, rental or hire purchase.

The contract value thresholds are ECU 200,000, and ECU 130,000 where GATT rules apply. In general, all purchases by central government departments are under GATT rules, so the smaller figure of ECU 130,000 will usually prevail. At either figure, however, meeting public supplies is very much within the abilities of small to medium-sized EC companies, and not just the larger ones.

Certain practices of using valuation of leases, rental and hire purchase agreements for the purposes of splitting the value threshold, to reduce it, have been proscribed to reinforce the prohibition of splitting contracts to evade the legislation.

Only the following types of procurement by public utilities are excluded:

1. Procurement by land, air, sea or inland water carriers – that is their own procurement.
2. Contracts concerning the production, transport and distribution of drinking water.
3. Procurement by public authorities whose principal activity is the production and distribution of energy or the provision of a public telecommunications network.

EC-wide competitive tendering and advertising in the *Official Journal Supplement* are required. There is a prescribed format for the layout and content of the tender notices, and there are three models for open, restricted and negotiated tenders. Pre-information procedures and the contract award information are also given.

In the matter of technical specifications, the rules are very similar to those for public works, but perhaps even more important, as most supplies concern products which will have standards applied to them. What was a recommendation to use EC standards in the original directive had become an obligation by 1992. Purchasing entities are obliged to define technical specifications by reference to national standards 'implementing European standards'. Once again this should be automatic as each national standards authority is, or has been, in the process of harmonizing its standards with the European standards, but one should always check for particular requirements with one's local standards agency. The technical specification can refer to 'common technical specifications' which can also be established by reference to the home standards agency.

In the absence of European standards or common technical specifications, purchasers may refer, subject to the principles of equivalence and mutual recognition of national technical specifications, to other documents. In that case they are recommended to refer (in order) to national standards implementing international standards and to other national standards.

In certain cases purchasers may depart from the general rule, but in those cases must justify doing so in their internal documentation and in the tender notice. These cases are where:

- The standards do not exist for establishing conformity or no satisfactory means of establishing conformity exist.
- Applying the rule would run counter to the Community provisions for telecommunications.
- It would oblige the purchaser to accept products incompatible with equipment already in use or would entail disproportionate costs or disproportionate technical difficulties.
- The project is genuinely innovative, making reference to existing standards inappropriate.

Tendering procedures

The amending directive elevates open tendering to the rule and restricts the use of other procedures. This is based on the EC experience that only open tenders are likely to provide equal opportunities for suppliers in all member states to bid for government contracts and are therefore the best way of opening up procurement to EC-wide competition. The open tenders are also the most 'open' in the sense of transparency and visibility.

Selective or restricted tendering is therefore an option only in justified cases, such as where the value of the contract does not warrant the procedural costs of open tender or where the product is too specific for open tender. All purchasers of selective or restrictive tenders, however, have to report on them to the Commission, explaining why the procedure was justified, and giving values, quantities, the number of suppliers asked to bid, and so on, thus ensuring a monitoring scheme.

It has also become very difficult to award contracts with no competitive bidding or in so called 'single tenders'. Both here and in the cases of negotiated tenders, reports must also be drawn up, as with the restricted above.

In open tenders the closing date must not be less that 52 days from dispatch of the tender notice from publication in the *Official Journal*. For restricted or selective tenders the closing dates for receipt of applications must be no less than 37 days from dispatch of tender notice, and there must not be less than 40 days between submission of bids and the sending of invitations to tender.

To summarize the three kinds of procedures:

- 'Open' are those where all interested parties can apply.
- 'Restricted' are when only those invited by the contracting authorities may submit tenders.
- 'Negotiated' are those chosen by the contracting authority and then negotiated with.

The two following sections explain the circumstance in which negotiation can be used:

Circumstances in which negotiation with individual suppliers without competitive tendering or advertising is allowed

1. Where no suitable supplier was found in a previous open or restricted tender because only irregular bids were received or because the bids submitted were unacceptable under national provisions that are consistent with the Community rules on public sector procurement, provided that the original terms for the contract are not substantially altered and that the purchaser includes in the negotiations all the firms not disqualified or eliminated for failure to meet the criteria for general suitability, financial standing and technical capacity which in the tender submitted bids in accordance with the formal requirements of the tendering procedures.
2. Where no bids at all were received in response to a previous open or restricted tender, provided that the original terms for the contract are not substantially altered and that the procurer sends the Commission a report.
3. Where the product is manufactured purely for the purposes of research, experiment, study or development; this provision does not include volume production to establish commercial viability or to recover research and development costs.
4. Where, for technical or artistic reasons or because of the

existence of exclusive rights, there is only one supplier in the Community able to supply the products.

5. In cases of extreme urgency resulting from unforeseen circumstances not attributable to the action of the purchaser, where the time limits laid down in the competitive tendering procedures cannot be observed.

6. For additional deliveries by the original supplier required either as part replacement of regular supplies or equipment, or to extend existing supplies or equipment, where a change of supplier would compel the contracting authority to acquire equipment having different technical characteristics which would result in incompatibility or disproportionate technical difficulties of operation or maintenance; the term of such contracts and of similar recurrent contracts may not, in general, exceed three years.

Circumstances in which negotiation with individual suppliers without competitive tendering but after advertising is allowed

Where no suitable supplier was found in a previous open or restricted tender because only irregular bids were received or because the bids submitted were unacceptable under national provision with the Community rules on public sector procurement, and the purchaser does not wish to include in the negotiations all suppliers not disqualified or eliminated on the grounds of general suitability, financial standing or technical capacity who in the previous tender submitted offers in accordance with the formal requirement of the tendering procedures. The original terms for the contract must not have been substantially altered.

In cases of urgency when observance of the normal time limit is not practical an accelerated form of restricted tender can be employed with shorter than normal time limits permitted. Purchasers must be able to prove the need for urgency.

In these 'accelerated' cases, the closing date for receipt of applications to bid must be not less than twelve days from the dispatch of the tender notice for publication in the *Official Journal*; additional information concerning the tender documents is to be sent no more than four days before the closing date for receipt of bids; while the closing date for the receipt of bids must be not less than ten days from the dispatch of the invitations to tender.

Finally, under the accelerated procedure, the most rapid means must be used for communicating applications and invitations to tender.

The rules for selection of contractors

The rules as to who may participate are very similar to those for the bidders in public works contracts covered in the last chapter and will not be repeated in full here. The rules for checking financial standing and for disqualification shown in the previous chapter can be used here. On the question of technical competence, however, the emphasis is somewhat different as the bidder is more likely to be a manufacturer than a contractor.

The evidence required of the supplier's technical competence must be stated in the tender notice and may not go beyond that needed for the purposes of the contract. The directives are fairly specific and give examples of evidence such as previous deliveries of products over three years, a description of the plant, details of technical resources, conformity to standards, quality management, and certifications. This is where accreditation to ISO 9000 is a great help, as it is an overall quality management certification, and is equivalent to EN 29000, the official EC standard.

The criteria for the award of contracts is as follows:

- Either the lowest price only; or
- when the award is made to the most economically advantageous tender, using such criteria as running costs, quality, delivery, aesthetic and functional characteristics, after sales service and technical support.

The contracting authorities must state in the contract documents or contract notice all the criteria they intend to apply to the award where possible in descending order of importance.

Provision of information

Wherever a contracting authority intends to spend ECU 750,000 or more in a year in a product area, it must give notice of this as soon as possible after the commencement of the financial year by means of a notice published in the *Official Journal*. This is extremely important for potential suppliers, as virtually all supplies are recurring or continuous.

There is a model tender notice available. The contracting authority must also publish the results of awards. Yearly, not later than 31 October, member states must report to the Commission detailing the number and value of contracts above the threshold, and in the case of central government also the value below the threshold. This last, presumably, to reveal trends towards splitting.

A useful timetable

The following timetables are suggested in the EC publication entitled *Public Procurement and Construction – Towards an Integrated Market*.

Timetable of the bidding process

Open tenders

- Immediately request tender documents and additional documentation. The authority awarding the contract is obliged under the EC rules to supply the tender documentation within four working days of receiving the request.
- Ask for any further information you need in connection with tender documents as soon as possible. The authority is obliged to supply information not later than six days before the closing date.
- Prepare the information and supporting documents you have to submit with your bid.
- Send off your bid by the closing date stated in notice.

Minimum period to be allowed until the closing date from dispatch of tender notice to the *Official Journal* publisher – 52 days.

Restricted (selective) tenders and contracts advertised before negotiation

- Apply to bid by letter or by telephone, telex, telefax or telegram (confirmed by letter) by the closing date stated in notice.
- Wait for invitation to tender, which must be accompanied by tender documents and additional documentation.

Minimum period to be allowed until closing date for application to bid from dispatch of tender notice to *Official Journal* publisher – 37 days.

- Ask for any further information you need in connection with tender documents as soon as possible. The authority awarding the contract is obliged under the EC rules to supply information not later than six days before the closing date for bids.
- Prepare the information and supporting documents you have to submit with your bid.
- Send off your bid by the closing date stated in notice.

Minimum period to be allowed until closing date for bids (restricted tenders only) from dispatch of invitations – 40 days.

'Accelerated' procedure in restricted tenders and for contracts advertised before negotiation

- Apply to bid by letter or by telephone, telex, telefax or telegram (confirmed by letter) by the closing date stated in notice.
- Wait for invitation to bid, which must be accompanied by tender documents and additional documentation.

Minimum period to be allowed until closing date for applications to bid from dispatch of tender notice to *Official Journal* publisher – 15 days.

- Ask for any further information you need in connection with tender documents as soon as possible. The authority awarding the contract is obliged under the EC rules to supply information not later than six days before the closing date for bids.
- Prepare the information and supporting documents you have to submit with your bid.
- Send off your bid by the closing date stated in notice.

Minimum period to be allowed until closing date for bids (restricted tenders only) from dispatch of invitations – 10 days.

CHAPTER 8

The EC Market for Services

The last three chapters have dealt with public procurement, and the last area of public procurement opened up to transnational suppliers was in fact services. This chapter, however, deals with services in general in the internal market, as this is such a large and important sector. The services element is, however, enormous in public procurement also, so this will be dealt with first. The rules governing the technicalities of doing business with public buyers have already been dealt with (in Chapters 6 and 7) so some information specific to services will now be given.

The services element is being described as dramatic in its potential in the newly opened up public procurement sector of the internal market. The purchases of services are considerable both in size and in their potential for suppliers of all sizes. They account for no less than 20 per cent of total public sector purchasing, and apply to all public bodies, central, regional, local, state enterprises, and public authorities.

A public service contract is a contract for pecuniary interest concluded in writing between a supplier and a contracting authority. While it covers a huge range of services, from PR to architecture, it excludes arbitration and conciliation services, acquisition of programming material by broadcasters, contracts for the purchase, lease or rental of, or concerning rights on, land, existing buildings or other immovable property, contracts concerning primary issues of government bonds and other activities in the area of public debt management, and, finally, public service concessions.

The exclusion of broadcast material is interesting, as it probably reflects the need for editors of public broadcast services to maintain total freedom over the acquisition of creative material, and the inability of any tendering systems to do justice to artistic creativity. This is the first of several examples where creativity triumphs over compliance with price thresholds and the letter of the law. This is most interesting for here at last is one area of opportunity in the internal market not constrained with rules and regulations, except, that is, for the editorial constraints.

The thresholds beyond which the rules apply are ECU 200,000 plus VAT, and ECU 100,000 for annual insurance premiums. Certain architectural and engineering services which involve the complete design of work worth ECU 5,000,000 plus VAT also come within the rules.

The rules lay down the types of tender procedure, advertising, selection, award of contracts, and the provision of information. France serves as an excellent model for selling into the EC public procurement market, for services as well as the other categories.

French calls for tenders tend to be well detailed and easily understood, such as calls for architectural plans for the City of Nice, turnkey electrical and plumbing design for the schools of Provence. All stages of product development and services are sourced from research and prototypes, to actual manufactured product, maintenance, and all related and other services.

The needs can be divided into four categories:

1. Services connected with building and civil engineering.
2. Industrial machinery services (in aeronautics, mechanics and electronics).
3. Intellectual services, including research and development.
4. Services related to the supply of everyday goods and needs.

Information is available in both advertisements and official guides.

The advertisements carry details of contracts on offer, and the details of contracts awarded. Official advertisements are found in:

- *Le Bulletin Officiel des Annonces des Marches Publics* (Official Bulletin of Public Contract announcements).
- The *Official Journal* of the EC.
- Specific administration or technical journals.
- Minitel.
- TED: Tenders Electronic Daily, an online electronic database, which is the computerized version of the *Official Journal*.
- Official Guides, published by specific departments.

To summarize these, all that one needs to know can be obtained either by reading the printed *Official Journal* each day, or by looking at its electronic version over TED. Both are available at the local EC offices of each country, or in one's own office if subscribed for.

The Defence and Post and Telecommunications Ministries represent 82 per cent of the markets. For international services, the state is a medium-sized buyer, interested mainly in naval construction, aircraft and weapons on the one hand, and services, such as telecommunications, on the other. Communities (communes) are the most important buyers. There are 36,000 communes in France. The collectives are mostly concerned with engineering products and services, and building and public works. The 99 departments and 26 regions represent respectively 17 per cent and 1 per cent of the market.

Public companies are mostly concerned with the following sectors:

- Food and natural resources.
- Electronics, pharmaceutical and chemicals.
- International services.
- Engineering products and services.

Companies trying to enter the French public procurement services market may encounter a variety of obstacles such as differences in language, administrative systems, and requirements of local clients. Some procurement agencies are less open to foreign competition than others, particularly in the case of local collectives (communities, regions, departments), who will often opt for a local supplier who contributes to the local economy, rather than a non-local (French or foreign) supplier. The conditions for local collective contracts, as

opposed to state procurement contracts and public enterprise contracts, are not always perfectly clear.

Often a public procurement agency will have an established relationship with a supplier. In this instance, it is difficult for other companies (French or foreign) to enter the market. Also of importance is the proximity of the contractor. For the regular supply of everyday goods and services, a public procurement agency will prefer someone who can deliver rapidly. Also, in the case of complex services, such as software, the purchaser may prefer a nearby supplier who can maintain the service without delay.

Much of what has been said above for the public procurement markets is also true of the EC private sector services market. For the exporter to Europe, services tend to be of high value-added content, of a sophisticated nature, employ skilled and highly educated people, and be very profitable. One huge market is the European information services market, which the EC has found to be a fragmented market full of linguistic, regulatory and technical barriers, which in its view acted as impediments to free trade. This area has consequently attracted EC attention and assistance. Legal problems have been seen to account for many of the barriers.

We find information technology among the large markets for services, covering all areas of activity from facilities management and disaster recovery to programming. Close on its heels is the ever growing market for telecommunications services, which embraces turnkey projects and advanced research and development work in areas like broadband communications. A very important point here is that many IT and telecommunications research projects may attract EC Framework grants, so that an ideal approach for a service provider might be to offer support which may also be EC-funded. This makes the prospect very attractive for the customer who may need the research but is being forced to employ the kind of outsourcing techniques which we will discuss in Chapter 10.

Training is a huge market in the 1990s internal market where worker training is compulsory under health and safety regulations and mandatory under such standards and regulations as ISO 9000, BS 7750 and the Eco-audit. One area worth close scrutiny is that of multimedia for training workers at their workstations. While the workstation is expanding the market for training, one must not assume that it is leaving the seminar or classroom behind, as multimedia will enhance training there also.

Above all, management consultancy services appear to be going transnational in Europe with the trend towards large practices, many incorporating accountancy. While benefiting from economies of scale, these large practices can suffer from the inability to adapt as fast as their smaller competitors, and smallness is not a disadvantage in the internal market for services. It is particularly interesting to see the larger consultancies now trying to get onto the environmental bandwagon where smaller companies can excel.

Banks are going transnational with their services, while transport companies are already in a global business, and EDI by its very nature has to be EC-wide also.

One of the most exciting services in Europe is information itself, particularly about the kinds of opportunities and regulations discussed in this book. TED with its published daily tenders is a good example, and there is even a market for refining TED to suit local territories and kinds of companies, especially small and medium-sized enterprises (SMEs), especially if one may offer additional commentary such as the likelihood of repeat orders, who else might want the product or service and what standards or specifications are involved.

Publishing itself continues to be in demand, but in the management and training areas it must accommodate such technological developments as video and interactive multimedia, as well as video-conferencing. CD-ROM, in particular, is making information available side by side with training at the workstation. Several large publishers are now producing CD-ROM versions (that is on compact disc) of the kinds of database discussed in this book. Information itself is big business in the internal market – as a journalist, this writer has been experiencing more and more demand from newspapers and specialist magazines for information about EC programmes, opportunities and regulations.

CHAPTER 9

EC Grants

Some member states have better records than others in obtaining a fair share of EC funding for industrial projects. At the time of writing, Robert Jackson, Parliamentary Secretary, Office of Public Service and Science in the UK, was critical of the fact that as many as 60 per cent of the top 100 UK R&D spending companies had never participated in EC research programmes. The main reason for this is probably a lack of knowledge of what is available. The UK research community, mostly based in the universities, has a good record, but this makes the situation all the stranger as the academics cannot be fully exploiting the industry links.

One may be forgiven for being confused about what kinds of funds are available from the EC, as the situation is indeed very confusing. This chapter is an attempt to describe the programmes with the most relevance to industry. The next chapter deals with those programmes specifically aimed at small and medium-sized enterprises (SMEs).

Apart from social and other schemes which supply funds for training, health and major items of national infrastructure, and apart from large sums in the poorer countries channelled through local organizations in the form of grants, the funds of most relevance to companies are those involving technology. There are two main sources of these funds.

The first of these are the Structural Funds or the Regional Funds, also called the Community Support Funds. These support agriculture, the social scheme, and the ERDF, the European Regional Development Fund. Under the ERDF there are a number of industry programmes, which are specific to poorer countries such as Ireland and Portugal. In Ireland these are, perhaps appropriately, named PAT – Programmes of Advanced Technology. In Portugal, there are similar programmes under different names. These two, which are of similar nature, are mentioned here first, and they may have only a limited interest for private companies as they do not involve any finance going directly to companies. They can, however, create opportunities for companies or consultants operating in these countries. The main programmes are in the areas of advanced manufacturing technology (AMT), bioresearch, optronics, power electronics, advanced materials, telecoms, sensors, software, executive information systems, and multimedia.

The PATs are funded through the offices of local ministries, 75 per cent from EC structural funds and 25 per cent for the central exchequer. The actual research work is usually carried out in universities with links with industry. Typically, the opportunities are to avail of new technologies for research, prototypes and product development. Examples might include an optronics laboratory carrying out research work for an electronics manufacturer, or a number of engineering companies participating in an AMT programme to learn more about linking, through JIT say, with major multinational customers.

The most important point about such projects within the Structural Funds is that they are really aimed at establishing a science and technology (S&T) infrastructure in the form of buildings, laboratories, staff and equipment. They do not fund actual research, so companies can be involved only by using the subsequent programmes which are carried out in the university-based facilities set up under the schemes, or by buying time in the facilities before embarking upon expensive capital acquisitions.

Direct funding for companies mostly comes through the next set of programmes called 'Framework'.

Between 1990 and 1994, the EC will have given nearly ECU 5,700 million in research grants to work in information and communications technologies, industrial and materials technologies, energy, life sciences and technologies, environment, and human capital and mobility. This is the so-called Third Framework Programme.

The third programme runs from 1990 to 1994 and involves fifteen specific programmes. These programmes overlap under a principle called rolling programme planning and at the time of writing the Fourth Framework Programme was being planned. A general overview of the programme is shown in Table 9.1.

TABLE 9.1

Area	Proportion of total budget
Information and communications technologies	38.9%
Industrial and materials technologies	15.6%
Environment	9.1%
Life sciences and technologies	13.0%
Energy	14.3%
Human capital and mobility	9.1%

The last ECU 3,200 million of the total of ECU 5,700 million will be spent in the years 1993 and 1994. Any person may apply to be grant-aided in a relevant research project, but the usual legal status is a company, a university or a private or public research institute. It is nearly always essential to have a partner from another member state to ensure cross-border cooperation. There may be more than one partner, although more than three might be considered too many. Small and medium-sized enterprises (SMEs) are favoured.

An SME, in the eyes of the EC, has less than 500 employees, a net turnover of less than ECU 38,000,000, and has no more than one third of its shares owned by a parent company or financial institution. In the past, much investment was restricted to those companies which had their own research capabilities, including the SMEs, but this is changing and in this respect 200 Euro-Information Centres have been set up to advise SMEs on opportunities and the submission of proposals in the member states. These may also call on consultants, and the local EC offices make lists of consultants available.

In the area of industrial and materials technology, there is also a cooperative programme for small companies, called CRAFT, Cooperative Research Action Programme, which allows those with no research facilities to pool resources and share joint research projects with third parties, such as larger partners, research institutes or universities. As many as ten to twenty companies can be involved and the red tape is minimized. For information on CRAFT, contact:

Robert Jan Smits,
Commission of the European Communities,
D6 XII
200, Rue de la Loi
B-1044 Brussels
Fax: +32/2/2 362007

It may actually work to the advantage of a large company to have an SME partner, as this will be looked on favourably, so the best advice would appear to be that unless one is in a CRAFT-type arrangement and does not have one's own research facilities, look for a large partner, not another small one. Ultimately of course, the correct partner is more important than the EC grant.

There are four kinds of EC support available, and these are as follows:

1. Contract research with cost sharing.
2. Concentration of research activities.
3. The Community's own research.
4. Bursaries and subsidies.

Contract research with cost sharing

This is the norm, the most popular, covering about 80 per cent of projects, with the Community paying up to 50 per cent of research costs, and, remember, that such costs include salaries and may be for work that one intends to do anyway, including new product or process development, although the last do not qualify if they are at the market-ready stage.

Concentration of research activities

This is where the EC does not pay for research but for such administrative costs as travel and meetings. This is meant chiefly for the coordination of national research programmes.

The Community's own research

The EC has four sites within its Joint Research Centre (JRC) and these are at Ispra in Italy, Geel in Belgium, Petten in the Netherlands and Karlsruhe in Germany. The JRC which formerly handled nuclear research under the Euratom Treaty now also carries out research into environmental protection, safety and satellite remote sensing. It engages in joint projects with industry and is open to research. The contact for JRC is:

> François Lafontaine
> Commission of the European Communities
> D6 XII – Joint Research Centre
> 200, Rue de la Loi,
> B-1049 Brussels

Bursaries and subsidies

For the training and education of both young and experienced scientists in the disciplines covered by the Third Framework Programme, the Commission awards bursaries and subsidies, specially at post-doctoral level. They must be citizens of the EC or certain EFTA countries and cannot be nationals of the country of the host institution or have been working there for more than two years prior to the date of the submission of the application, except in certain cases such as the JRC. The duration of the bursary can be from six months to two years and payments can be between ECU 1,500 to 3,000 per month. The receiver of a bursary holder, which can be a university, a private institution or a company can also receive a subsidy of either ECU 5,000 or 10,000 per annum.

Staying in touch

The following remarks have much in common with those concerning getting information about public procurement calls for tenders. By the time one reads about a call for proposals under the Framework Programme, it may be too late to do all that is necessary. There are two main ways of staying in touch and knowing in advance what calls are coming up. The first is through national contact points or programme consultants, the second by reading the relevant material, both in hard copy and electronically. While the former can be good, and even exceptional, it may equally be very poor, as it depends very much on the quality and availability of the named local contact. Any journalist working in this area will know that there are some national representatives of EC programmes who should never have been given the job, as they are not available for practical purposes. The problem is compounded if one should contact the EC directly as one is referred back to the poor local contact point. On the other hand some national contact persons are quite good and provide important inside information. The national contact person for any programme will be found by contacting a local Euro-Information Centre. It is, however, recommended that other sources in printed and electronic form are consulted.

The best of these by far is the *Official Journal* of the European Communities, parts of which are published daily. The relevant parts of this will be found in two formats, in the original printed hard copy form at the local EC office or Euro-Information Centre, or over the Tenders Electronic Daily (TED) database, discussed in the chapters on public procurement and in Chapters 22 and 25. There is also a database called CORDIS, which specializes in bringing all information concerning research and technology into one place (see Chapter 22). The first indication of a potential research project will be the news in the *Official Journal* that a proposal is, or has been, prepared by the Commission. The *Official Journal* can be subscribed for, in hard copy, directly obtained electronically over TED, seen in an EC office or in any state industry support agency, or purchased from government publications offices. The relevant sections are:

- Part C: Notice of the Commission's proposals for new research programmes and calls for proposals.
- Part L: Council decisions on research programmes.
- Part S: Known as the 'Supplement' – calls for proposals.

The newsletter *Innovation and Technology Transfer* also carries full information on coming and current proposals and the Commission also hosts national information events to publicize programmes.

The research is expected to relate to the so called pre-competitive phase, that is not to products or processes that are market-ready, although future developments will be in the mind of the proposer. This is because the EC does not want to distort competition by unfairly helping one producer against the competition.

The general criteria involved in selecting projects might be summarized as follows:

- The proposals should relate to the programme outlined in the *Official Journal*.
- It should involve cross-border participation, scientific and technical innovation and quality, relate to a pre-competitive stage, and have a European dimension.
- You must demonstrate an ability to finance 50 per cent of the costs, the capacity to carry out the project, be able to utilize the results and have the technical competence.

Three other criteria help and these are: being an SME, doing something good for the environment, having a partner from Greece, Spain, Portugal or Ireland. Where other criteria are equal, the Commission chooses on the basis of the last three.

So, how do you begin your project proposal? If the reader is experienced, he or she will not need this advice, but if not, the first sensible step having established that there is potential from a particular source, is to look for a partner. That partner may also be inexperienced, but if it is a university, or a research establishment, it will already be very experienced in dealing with proposals. So think backwards. What university or research establishment in another EC country would be interested in a partner, especially if you are an SME? That choice will be helped greatly by the development area chosen. So one way is to approach one of your local universities or research centres where that subject, for example, environmental control, is studied, ask for the names of contacts in a cross-border institute, and then contact that institute. If one is looking for a company, one may use a variety of methods, including accessing 400 business consultants, who may have suitable clients, through the EC Office for Business Cooperation.

Once a suitable partner is found, one member of the partnership must act as the coordinator, who will be both project manager and reporter. At this point, we introduce the concepts of contractor, associated contractor and subcontractors. The contractor signs the contract with the EC, the associated contractor participates in the financing and execution of the project, while a subcontractor is an outsider hired by the other two parties. Subcontracts above ECU 100,000 or exceeding 20 per cent of total costs must be agreed by the Commission, but in general dealings between parties are not the concern of the Commission.

The allowable costs in the project embrace personnel, wear and tear of equipment at 20 per cent per annum, of computers, the cost of which may not exceed ECU 10,000, 33 per cent per annum, consumables, subcontractors fees, unreserved VAT and other duties, and overheads. Great flexibility is allowed in transferring costs from areas under utilized to those suffering overruns; also, one is allowed to carry forward unused expenditure from year to year and between partners.

The proposal simply follows the outline laid down in the published *Call for Proposals* and in a detailed information pack which comes on application with the proposal forms. When the proposal is accepted the Commission invites you to enter into contract negotiations and issues a contract. A model contract proposed by the Commission is discussed in the next section.

The model contract

Only what appear to be useful points are included here.

The work programme which is submitted in an annex to each contract allows one to breakdown an amount of work into a series of 'milestones' and funds are agreed to cover work up to each such milestone. There are advance payments and periodic payments. Ten per cent, or ECU 500,000, whichever is the lower, is retained until all contracted reports or other 'deliverables' are provided to the Commission. The results are the property of contractors. Contractors who benefit from the grants may employ subcontractors without permission from the Commission, where the values subcontracted do not exceed ECU 100,000. Conditions regarding the confidentiality of the results and publicity are agreed in each contract.

Allowable costs include: labour, overheads, travel and subsistence, equipment, consumables, computing, outside help, sundries, and taxation and duties.

An actual model contract is available, entitled *Model Contract for Community Activities in the Fields of Research and Technological Development*. It can be obtained from Directorate General XII Science, Research and Development.

Details of Framework programmes

The Framework programmes are 5-year R&D plans offering many opportunities for participation by companies, institutions and individuals. These are now looked at in some detail. This information was kindly given by the European Commission. Fuller information can be obtained from the Commission's own published book *EC Research Funding 3rd Framework* (subtitled A Guide for Applicants) and there should be a 4th Framework version available from late 1993.

Important note

This writer has written extensively in newspapers and magazines on EC calls for proposals and has found that only in a newspaper or monthly journal can one give sufficient notice of opportunities, so short are the lead times. It cannot be done in a book. The examples now given refer to 1990–1994 projects in the Third Framework Programme. Readers will be looking at these pages during 1993 and 1994 and it is therefore important, when following up any of these, to ask not just what calls for proposals may be left within the remaining time period, but what new elements for the Fourth Framework are being 'rolled in', and, just as important, what new programmes. Those which are listed below, however, are likely to be around for a while, but, if not, do not be put off – ask if they have been renewed under a different title.

Information technology

The main programme here is ESPRIT, which is the specific research and technological development programme in the field of information technologies. This huge programme has received ECU 1,400 million from the EC for 1990–1994. The specific areas are:

- Microelectronics.
- Information processing systems and software.
- Advanced business and home systems – peripherals.
- Computer integrated manufacturing and engineering.
- Basic research.

Communications technologies

The one programme here is IBC, the development of integrated broadband communication. This replaced RACE and is receiving ECU 484 million. The specific areas are:

- Broadband communications.
- Intelligent networks.
- Mobile and personal communications.
- Image and data communications.
- Integrated service technologies.
- Advanced communication equipment.
- Test infrastructure and interworking.

Telematics systems

The objective of this programme is to provide the conceptual, technological and prenormative basis for the gradual implementation of trans-European telematics service networks, in areas such as administrations, transport, health, distance learning, libraries, linguistics, rural areas. This is worth ECU 376 million. The specific areas are:

- The establishment of trans-European networks between administrations.
- V12 – customs, emergency services, social services.
- Transport services (DRIVE); using advanced IT and communications.
- Healthbase (AIM); the development of harmonized applications of information and communications technology.
- Flexible and distance learning (DELTA); strategies and developments.
- Libraries; systems of user access, international interconnection; linguistics, technology and pilot applications; telematics for rural areas (DRA).
- Applications, implementation strategies.

Industrial and materials technologies

This was formerly BRITE/EURAM, and has an objective to contribute to the regeneration of European manufacturing industry by basic technical research and new technology, and to help SMEs to become involved in research. It is worth ECU 663 million. The specific areas are:

- Materials. This includes raw materials, recycling, structural materials, such as ceramics, functional materials and mass commodity, such as packaging and new construction.
- Design and manufacturing. This includes design of products and tools, techniques, complex components, manufacturing techniques, and product life cycle.
- Aeronautics. This includes aircraft operation, structures, materials avionic systems.

Measurement and testing

This is to improve measurements, testing techniques and chemical analyses and to achieve the mutual recognition of laboratories. It is worth ECU 47 million. The specific areas are:

- Regulations and Directives.
- Harmonization of test methods – viz. food controls.
- Sectoral testing problems.
- New standardized testing methods.
- Common means of calibration.
- Development of standards and reference materials.
- Development of new methods of measurements.
- Measurement principles, leading to new types of instruments.

Environment

This area should expand. Its objective is to develop the scientific and technological knowledge that the Community needs to carry out its role concerning the environment. This is worth ECU 261 million. The specific areas are:

- Exploration of global environmental change.
- Technologies and engineering for the environment.
- Research on economic and social aspects of environmental issues.
- Technological and natural risks.

Likely new areas are halogens in the atmosphere, the fight against desertification, and the avoidance, recycling, treatment and disposal of waste.

Marine science

The previous programme here was MAST. Its objective is to contribute to establishing a scientific and technological basis for the exploration, exploitation, management and protection of European coastal waters and the seas surrounding the EC member states. It is worth ECU 103 million. The specific areas are:

- Marine science.
- Coastal zone science and engineering.
- Marine technology.
- Supporting initiatives – viz. information systems, standards, training.
- Large scale multidisciplinary projects – viz. Mediterranean projects.

Biotechnology

The objective here is to reinforce basic biological knowledge as a common and integrated foundation needed for applications in agriculture, industry, health, nutrition and the environment. This is worth ECU 162 million. The specific areas are:

- Molecular approaches.
- Cellular and organism approaches.
- Ecology and population biology.

The objectives are to reinforce European knowledge in biotechnology as a foundation required for applications in agriculture, industry, health and the environment. This programme is the successor to the BEP, BAP and BRIDGE programmes.

Agriculture

This follows several previous programmes, such as ECLAIR, FLAIR, FAR, FOREST, and Agriculture. The objective is to upgrade and diversify agricultural and silvicultural products, to enhance the competitiveness of agricultural and agri-food undertakings, to contribute to better rural and forestry management, and to ensure proper protection for the environment. This is worth ECU 330 million. The specific areas are:

- Primary production in agriculture, horticulture, forestry, fisheries and aquaculture (including environmentally friendly production systems).
- Inputs in agriculture, horticulture, forestry, fisheries and aquaculture – viz. improvements.
- Processing of biological raw materials from agriculture, horticulture, forestry, fisheries and aquaculture.
- End use and products, including hygiene and safety, packaging.

Biomedical/health research

This is to contribute to improving the efficiency of medical and health research and development in the member states, particularly through coordination and cooperation. It is worth ECU 132 million. The specific areas are:

- Coordinate research.
- Major health and disease problems – viz. AIDS, cancer.
- Human gene analysis.
- Biomedical ethics.

Life sciences for developing countries

This was called STD, and is now the further strengthening of research capacity in both the developing countries and the member states in areas defined as having priority for Third World development, or the improvement of coordination with the EC. It is worth ECU 110 million. The specific areas are:

- Improvement of living conditions.
- Development of agricultural products with high economic value.
- Improvement of health.
- Health care systems.
- Nutrition.

At the time of writing there were more calls for proposals planned during 1993.

Energies (non-nuclear)

This replaces JOULE, and contributes to the development of new energy options that are both economically viable and environmentally safe, including energy saving technologies. This is worth ECU 155 million. Note that there is also a Thermie Programme (see Chapter 10). The specific areas are:

- Analyses of strategies and modelling.
- Minimum emissions from fossil sources (power production).
- Renewable energy sources.
- Geothermal energy and deep reservoir geology.
- Energy utilization and conservation.

Nuclear

There are two programmes – nuclear fission safety, worth ECU 36 million and controlled thermonuclear fusion, worth ECU 412 million, which is also known as the JET project. These are so specialized that they are not discussed in this book.

Human capital and mobility

This follows such previous programmes as SCIENCE and SPES, and its objective is to increase the human resources available for research and technological development which will be needed by the member states in the coming years. It is also concerned with the mobility of researchers and with the formation of networks. It is worth ECU 488 million. The specific areas are:

- The development of a Community system of research training.
- The creation and development of research cooperative networks
  – viz. at least five research teams in at least three countries.
- The establishment of access to large-scale scientific and technical facilities.
- Euroconferences.

Dissemination and exploitation of knowledge

This was, and has a parallel, in VALUE, and gives specific added value to all the R&D activities which are listed above in the Third Framework Programme. It is worth ECU 57 million. The specific areas are:

- Research-industry interface. New channels of information – viz. the CORDIS database.
- Interface between research and the scientific community.
- Interface between research and society – viz. communication with the public.

Conclusion

This chapter has discussed the main Framework Programme. The next chapter covers programmes specific to SMEs, while Chapter 25 lists other supports, including finance, and Appendix 3 gives supports available from the EC through national governments.

CHAPTER 10

Opportunities for Small and Medium-sized Enterprises

The SME, the small and medium-sized enterprise, is an important business entity in the European Community. A small business is defined as independent, employing fewer than 50 people and with a turnover of less than ECU 5,000,000 or a net capital below ECU 2,000,000. A small and medium-sized enterprise is defined as an independent business, no more than 25 per cent of the shares of which can be held by one or more large companies, that has no more than 250 staff, and either a turnover of less than ECU 20,000,000, or total assets net of depreciation less than ECU 10,000,000.

There are many opportunities for SMEs, some shared by all SMEs internationally, some specific to Europe. Most of this chapter will be taken up with a step by step list of EC programmes directed at SMEs, but first we will review the overall climate for these enterprises. Much of what is said here also relates to very small companies, and even to individuals, such as consultants.

Perhaps the greatest strengths of SMEs and small enterprises or groups of individuals are in their ease of movement and speed of response, particularly their ability to respond quickly to perceived opportunities. They do indeed lack capital, the ability to invest in long-term market analysis and economies of scale, but they can spot opportunities rapidly and operate free of red tape. Many of their individuals will not have to wait for top management approval in a world where reduced lead times and 'time compression' give one a market advantage. They can also practise a form of business integration, by embracing a number of functions, which would be found difficult by large companies.

In a number of European countries, particularly the smaller ones, and in a number of areas favoured by cohesion funds, SMEs are favoured for national state and EC grants. These grants may be directed towards R&D for product development, training, and employment. There will be no discrimination in public procurement, except where credibility is an issue, against smaller companies; indeed, European-oriented buyers may favour smaller enterprises. The Europartenariat programme favours at least one partner being an SME, and most MNCs like to deal with small companies.

There is a huge range of business open to the SME, and this may be broken down into the following main categories:

- Sub-supply of components.
- Own products manufacture.
- Services.
- Consulting and training.

The climate for the sub-supply of components is very good worldwide, and there is more about this in Chapter 11, Selling to the Multinational Corporations. The SME must ensure it adopts the necessary demands of selling to MNCs as discussed and as shown in the sample contracts and vendor assessments. A supplier of components may, of course, also sell to other non-MNCs, to public procurement bodies, and to other SMEs.

Many SMEs are product producers and exporters of their own products in their own right, although there is a tendency for these either to grow or to suffer destructive competition, or at least to experience takeover. These companies tend to have products in market niches, such as food or drink, or gifts, and both companies and products tend also to be of high-quality, and difficult to compete with.

The services area is, of course, absolutely huge and predominantly the milieu of the SME, ranging from translation to law, from PR to catering. Typical service areas traditionally outsourced are canteen, building maintenance, security, computing, transport, accountancy, legal and public relations.

Consulting and training are shared between the large international consultants and a huge number of individuals from authors to university professors. In this business, 'the early bird catches the worm', and one has to have a market edge by being well informed. Two extremely valuable areas of information for the EC market of the nineties are legislation and opportunities, the former, specifically, the legislation which affects the selling of products and services, the latter the opportunities which will follow original calls for proposals. Information on these subjects will be found in the chapters on the specific areas mentioned.

An area of great potential for SMEs is partnerships and there is a special EC programme for facilitating partnerships between SMEs, whose sizes, one must remember, may vary greatly. This is called the Europartenariat Programme.

During 1993, the eight and ninth meetings of Europartenariat took place. The meetings are private affairs between several hundred companies from two different regions in the Community. This is how it works (originating in regions such as Ireland, Spain, Wales, Portugal, East Germany and Greece).

The first phase is the selection of local companies on the basis of the industrial cooperation projects they propose to foreign entrepreneurs, their characteristics and past performance (technological level, exports turnover, and so on).

The second phase begins with the inclusion of the selected businesses and their proposals in a catalogue, which will be distributed not only in other EC countries but also in the EFTA nations, the Eastern and Central European (PECO) countries and those in the Mediterranean basin. A consultant organization is chosen in each country to promote the initiative in business circles and to collect the participation forms of the interested firms.

The third phase involves the actual organization of the two day meeting, where local firms are assigned individual stands and where they meet foreign entrepreneurs following a predetermined schedule, to discuss in greater detail the cooperation proposals outlined in the catalogue.

Experience indicates that each of the host country's businesses meets

an average of eight foreign firms. Consequently, the business en-
counters that occur during the two day meetings run into thousands
(2,500 in Wales and Portugal, over 4,200 in Germany), and a great many
cooperation agreements are finalized (on average 35 per cent of the
selected businesses sign an agreement).

Local state agencies and industrial and business associations also
become involved in both the host region where the events are held and
in the countries of the visiting companies. In the 1992 Mezzogiorno,
Southern Italy event, for example, the following agencies were involved.
Confidustria, the association of Italian private enterprises in the
industrial and business services fields. This has a membership of about
110,000 firms listed on a geographical basis and by production sectors.
Membership of Confidustria and its associations is free and voluntary.

IASM, the Institute of Assistance in the Development of Southern
Italy, is an Italian Government Agency dedicated to promotion of new
industrial projects, the provision of technical assistance and expert
advice to services firms, the implementation of integrated development
projects and the promotion and application of EC programmes.

Unioncamere/Mondimpresa are the names of the Italian chambers of
commerce system, which plays a central role in Italy's national and local
economy for the accomplishment of objectives of common interest to
the State and the business world. It offers an integrated network of
services available to businesses, especially small and medium-sized
firms, comprising administration, information, training, assistance and
promotion services to develop their business potential. It is not
articulated in a vertical structure but in the form of a network of
decentralized points extending all over Italy and thus in direct contact
with local business needs and trends.

Typical costs for the Italian event were £600 for companies employing
less than 250, £800 for larger companies. The fee included full return air
fare, attendance at a mission dinner in Milan, up to three nights hotel
accommodation, and itinerary preparation – up to one half day of Milan-
based staff's time in setting up appointments to meet appropriate
contacts. Detailed market research was also available at a fee. The
Europartenariat meetings were also arranged.

Finally, there is a list of consultants, with at least one in each member
state to help companies to participate in the programme. This can
change from event to event, so to find the appropriate person, contact
your local state export office or central chamber of commerce. Note,
that this also means there is an opportunity to be a consultant. There are
five consultants in the UK for example.

For more details and for precise information on past and future Europartenariat events one should contact either, or both, of the following: Mr Vincent Degert, EC – DG XVI, Rue Pére De Deken, Court St Michel, 1040-0 Bruxelles (tel: . . ./2953503) or Mr Geert Heikens, EC – DG XXIII, 200 Rue de la Loi, 1049 – Bruxelles (tel: . . ./2957335).

Outsourcing

The concept of outsourcing has been sweeping industry and is being adopted readily in Europe. It is the contracting out of one or more functions which are needed within an organization. It flies in the face of former perceived trends of global dominance by the MNCs, monopolies, cartels, and big business putting paid to small business. The very opposite is happening with outsourcing as more and more business is being handed over to outsiders.

Chapter 11, Selling to the Multinational Corporations, warns how not to benefit from outsourcing. One must be able to get on the same wavelength as the customer, in quality, environmental demands, JIT, EDI, or whatever else is demanded, but assuming that one is willing and able, the outsourcing trend is full of potential for business. A surprising range of services is outsourced, even research and development.

Hewlett Packard in Europe outsources, but it does not outsource what it calls its 'core competencies', that is the core business, which it does well, and does not want others to do. This would appear to make a lot of sense: what surgeon, artist, writer or architect would want to outsource his or her core competency. Amazingly, perhaps, many major manufacturers, including Hewlett Packard's own competitors, outsource the most basic of their core competencies. Companies like Apple outsource so much, from printed circuit boards to whole computers, that it is difficult to establish what they would not outsource. Virtually all computer manufacturers outsource peripherals, including screens and keyboards, and this is the same for most manufacturers of electronics, telecommunications, and electrical equipment.

Outsourcing is a growth business: at the time of writing, Digital was reporting that it was the fastest growth sector of the information technology market, between 20 per cent and 30 per cent annually. Digital also claimed that 80 per cent of the top 500 organizations would outsource at least one of their IT functions by 1996.

While the upsurge in outsourcing is new, the concept is quite old. Auditing and legal services have always been outsourced, as has much of transport, customs clearance, communications, and even data processing. Specialist services such as maintenance, buildings, security, canteen and training have had a long history of outsourcing.

Outsourcing has one very important potential advantage for the buyer – it can tap into a vein of creativity and innovation not found within the organization, especially if the supplier has other customers.

Digital recommends a service level agreement (SLA) between the provider of a service and users which quantifies the minimum acceptable level of service. It also warns against unspecified user expectations which can lead to disenchantment.

A potential supplier can influence the decision to outsource by selling the idea in the first instance to a prospective customer and then helping the decision to be made by assisting with the cost-benefit analysis. For this purpose the supplier needs to know what the steps are in the decision-making process. Here they are, roughly, and the similarity between them and any project will be noticeable.

- Generate the idea.
- Establish the current costs of the function under review.
- Estimate the cost trends and future costs.
- Analyse the staff position – is it difficult to obtain staff?
- Compare inhouse with outsource costs.
- Is it a core competence, and so what?
- What are the risks?
- Produce a proposal.

A very important point which must be considered in outsourcing is ownership. This is fairly straightforward where the outsourcing is for a component, and it will be covered by an agreement such as that shown in the Amdahl Life of Product Agreement in Appendix 1, but the issue of ownership is more complex where R&D or design work are outsourced, especially if these are in leading edge activities. Is the outsourcer working for competitors and, if so, is the work being done for you necessarily going to enhance that done for the competition?

This is a very difficult question made all the more difficult by the fact that some competitors are now forming alliances with each other. So great is the trend towards outsourcing and alliances that it will be necessary, during design and pre-production phases, for tight legal agreements on non-disclosure to be drawn up between customer and outsource, particularly where new technology and new product development are involved.

There are a number of outsource possibilities, however, where the value of the service supplied is so great that the customer will want it regardless of who else is buying it. These services include strategic planning, the analyses of market trends, evolving legislation, and trends in technology. If a small supplier can provide such strategic assistance as market and technical trends, for example, this may be a supplier's market.

We now move on to the major area of opportunities for SMEs in the internal market – the special EC programmes and grants for SMEs. Some of these will already have been covered in Chapter 9, EC Grants, but to ensure completeness, they will be mentioned here again, specifically in the context of SMEs.

Opportunities for small and medium-sized enterprises

The details of opportunities which now follow are based on an excellent analysis of EC grants possibilities appearing in a booklet published jointly by the international accounting and consulting firm KPMG and the Small Firms Association of the Confederation of Irish Industries. This work, published in late 1992, looks across the whole EC growth spectrum and extracts those possibilities of relevance to small and medium sized enterprises. It is therefore relevant to all such enterprises across the Community. The title of the study is *EC Grants Guide – a comprehensive guide to EC grants and support programmes aimed at small and medium-sized companies.*

Large companies will have the resources to study research grant possibilities in depth: this chapter, like the KPMG study, is intended as a simple guide for SMEs through the morass of EC possibilities to the availability of financial assistance from the Commission. Readers, particularly those in Spain, Portugal, Greece and Ireland, should bear in mind that individual member state support programmes and grant assistance, over and above these EC supports, are extra and are not listed here.

Other comments similar to those in Chapter 9 need to be made. At the time of writing the Third Framework Programme was beginning to be overlaid with the Fourth Framework Programme. Although a number of the projects here may already be fully subscribed at the time of writing, they are mentioned because they may be repeated, either as they are or in another format in the rest of the Third and all of the stages of the Fourth Programme.

The kinds of grants and assistance for SMEs are dealt with in three different places in this book. First, in this chapter, are the main grant programmes for business activities, mostly under the Framework Programme, directly accessible to SMEs; second, supports in the form of information, hand-holding, loans and capital are discussed in Chapter 25; and finally, other assorted EC grants which are administered through national government bodies are detailed in Appendix 3. Some of the grants which follow may also have to be cross-referenced to the previous chapter, as this chapter tries to avoid unnecessary repetition.

Agriculture

Agriculture, forests, fisheries and aquaculture. The programmes are CAMAR, ECLAIR, FLAIR, FAR and various forestry and biomass programmes. Most of these have the objective of upgrading and diversifying products, enhancing competitiveness and contributing to better management (including environmental management). The projects must be pre-competitive and involve researcher collaboration with industrial organizations. Fifty per cent funding is available. See also Chapter 9 for further details.

Brussels contact: M. D. Dessylas, Commission of the European Communities, DG VI/F/2.3, 130 Rue de la Loi, B-1049, Brussels.

BIOMED I

Biomedicine and health research

The aim is to improve the efficacy of medical and health research and development in member states, in particular, by better coordination of the member states' research and development activities and application of the results through Community cooperation and a pooling of resources. See also Chapter 9.

Biotechnology

To develop commercial applications in biotechnology. See also Chapter 9.

BRITE/EURAM II

The Community Research Programme on industrial technologies and new materials is designed to strengthen the scientific and technological base of European manufacturing industry. It intends to improve the capability of manufacturers, and in particular SMEs, to design and produce products that are highly competitive and environmentally and socially acceptable. It aims to assist manufacturing companies in reducing the product design cycle, total process time and throughput time, as well as assisting in the use of process technology and the application of procedures, ensuring high quality and cost effectiveness of products and components.

Duration: 1990–1994. EC contribution: ECU 663 million. See also under the heading Industrial and materials technologies in Chapter 9.

BRITE/EURAM II – CRAFT

To assist SMEs with limited or no research capability of their own.
Grant assistance: funding may be available as follows.

- Fifty per cent of the costs of the research project, costing ECU 0.4–1 million and lasting 1–2 years.
- Development grants of up to ECU 15,000 may also be available to companies where an initial outline proposal has been submitted and where further details are required in order to provide the Commission with a detailed proposal for inclusion under the CRAFT programme. In this case, assistance may be provided towards the costs of employing consultants, sourcing additional technical data, and so on.

Project eligibility: projects where several companies, in particular SMEs, who are all facing a technical problem involving one or several industries, join forces and award joint research contracts to third parties, such as commercial laboratories, universities or research institutes and/or companies.

Companies must be involved in manufacturing, mining, construction, process engineering, recycling, or related areas and have no inhouse research capability. Projects must involve at least:

1. Two SMEs established in different member states.
2. Four SMEs established in at least two different member states.

Companies must be independent of each other. Companies involved in scientific services, such as software companies, are not eligible. Development grants may be available to assist SMEs to move projects involving two SMEs to projects involving four SMEs.

BRITE/EURAM II – Feasibility grants

To assist SMEs in establishing the feasibility of a new device, process or concept with a view to preparing a proposal in the BRITE/EURAM context (see details above). The programme will assist SMEs to demonstrate to potential partners their capacity to contribute to a new project and prove their research capability.

Grant assistance: grants of up to 75 per cent to a maximum of ECU 30,000, may be available towards the costs of research projects undertaken within a 9 month period and which allow the company to collate the necessary information to formulate a full proposal under the main BRITE/EURAM programme.

Eligibility: restricted to SMEs involved in manufacturing, mining, construction, process engineering, recycling and related areas. There are no partnership agreements – individual companies can apply. Companies involved in scientific services, such as software companies are not eligible.

For training grants under BRITE/EURAM see Chapter 25.

DOSES II (Development of Statistical Expert Systems)

To promote the use of advanced techniques for processing statistical data, in particular the application of an expert system for the whole chain of statistical data processing. It hopes to lay the foundations for the development of expert systems in the various domains of statistics.

Duration: 1993 to an as yet unspecified date. Grant assistance: funding of up to 50 per cent may be available for:

- The organisation of coordinated projects.
- Research and development projects regarded as meriting priority in official statistics, such as the development of prototypes of statistical tools as a forecasting model or large surveys.

Application procedures: fixed calls for proposals are issued in the EC *Official Journal*. Beneficiaries: public authorities, universities and private enterprises. DOSES II is expected to focus more on private enterprises including SMEs.

Environmental research and development programme

This programme aims to offer technical and scientific support for the environmental policy of the Community and to increase the productivity of the Community's overall research through the coordination of national programmes in the environmental research area. The programme is a follow-up to STEP, EPOCH and HAZARD.

Duration: 1990–1994. EC contributions: ECU 260 million. See also under the heading Environment in Chapter 9.

ESPRIT III (European Strategic Programme of R&D in Information Technology)

To provide the European IT industry with the basic technologies to meet future competitive requirements; to promote European industrial co-operation in IT and to contribute to the development of internationally accepted standards.

Duration: 1990–1994. EC contribution: ECU 1,352 million. A budget of approximately ECU 400 million is expected for the second call for proposals. See also under the heading Information Technology in Chapter 9.

EUREKA

A programme designed to help European countries and companies to exploit and to keep abreast of emerging technologies. EUREKA interacts with companies and research institutes in EUREKA member countries and helps them pool their resources in the development of products, processes and services, having a worldwide market potential and based on advanced technology.

Contribution: ECU 1 billion. Assistance: the national Governments of the partners concerned decide whether support will be given and fix the extent of the subsidy. EUREKA provides a network of national offices for bringing partners together, encouraging the adoption of common standards, and so on. The national project coordinators through the EUREKA Secretariat in Brussels attempt to seek partners in other EUREKA countries. The EUREKA Secretariat has access to a databases with information on all current projects and projects in preparation.

Project eligibility: advanced R&D projects involving companies or research institutes from a minimum of two countries where the aim of the project is to secure a significant technological advance in the product, process and service concerned for which an available international market exists. Whereas EC research is mainly concerned with pre-competitive and basic research, EUREKA projects are nearer to the market.

EURET

For the stimulation of the economic efficiency, safety and environmental acceptability of transport and to ensure that the development of Community transportation (air, sea and land) will be capable of meeting increased demands resulting from the completion of the internal market.

EC contribution: ECU 25 million. Funds have been fully allocated. It is, however, anticipated that new funds will be allocated to this area in January 1994. Grant assistance: financial assistance may be available for:

- Cost-benefit analysis for new road construction.
- European rail traffic management.
- Design and assessment of vessel traffic management.
- Automatic air/ground data exchange for traffic management and the position of the air controller.
- Road safety of car and trailer trains and the driving safety of possible truck and trailer combinations.

It is anticipated that future funds will be focused on projects which include:

- Software – traffic statistics, traffic management, system analysis.
- Road building – improve quality, road construction techniques.

- Application of information technology, such as port management, air traffic control, freight management.

Euromanagement

Euromanagement for standards and certification was launched to cover
the area of standardization, certification and quality. It aims to assist
SMEs and craft trades to identify and evaluate the incidence of new
European requirements for standardization, certification and quality
which they will have to meet to benefit from the Single European
Market.

Procedure: fifty consultants and advisers selected from a call for
tenders throughout the member states each visit 10–15 SMEs to assess
their problems and requirements and to determine the actions which
need to be taken in the area of standardization and certification. This is
done according to a common methodology developed by a specialist
company. A private company has been selected to coordinate the
management and evaluation of the pilot project. The coordinator is
expected to finalize a methodology, plan a seminar and a training
manual for the fifty consultants or advisers chosen to carry out the
standardization and certification audits.

The first phase is over, but more action may follow.

Human capital and mobility

To increase the human resources available for research and technological development in Europe. It is an initiative built on training through
research collaboration. This takes over from the SCIENCE and SPEC
programmes and large scale scientific facilities.

Duration: 1991–1994. EC contribution: ECU 470 million. See also
under the heading Human capital and mobility in Chapter 9.

**IMPACT II (Programme for the Establishment of an
Information Services Market)**

To facilitate the establishment of an internal information services
market in Europe. It aims to reinforce the competitive capability of
European suppliers of information services, and to promote the use of

advanced information services in the Community. It also wishes to create an environment in which information can flow freely across national boundaries.

Duration: 1991–1995. EC contribution: ECU 64 million. Grant assistance: funding may be available as follows:

- Twenty-five to fifty per cent for shared cost contracts.
- One hundred per cent for service contracts.

Industrial research and development initiative

To enhance both the number and size of the product and process development projects undertaken by industry. The projects must be significant and key projects in establishing or maintaining a company's competitive advantage.

Duration: 1992–1993 (pilot phase). Grant assistance: grants of up to 50 per cent of qualifying expenditure will be available.

LEIs (Local Employment Initiatives)

Set up in 1984 to support and encourage entrepreneurial women to set up their own business cooperatives or other employment creation initiatives.

Duration: 1991–1995. EC contribution: ECU 1.5 million Grant assistance: grants of up to ECU 1,500 per full time job created may be provided. Maximum amount available to any one company: ECU 7,500. Project eligibility:

- Grants will be provided only to a business start-up.
- Businesses must create jobs for women – with preferences going to immigrant women, disabled, long-term unemployed and single parent mothers.
- A minimum of two full time jobs and a maximum of five full time jobs are eligible for support.
- Men may be employed by the business but the decision-making process must be undertaken by women staff.

Beneficiaries: business start-up situations or community initiatives involving women in management.

MEDIA (Action Programme to Promote the Development of the European Audio-Visual Industry)

The programme's aims are:

- To stimulate European film production and distribution across Europe.
- To contribute to the worldwide making of European productions.
- To promote new European communications technologies in film production and distribution.
- To improve the economic and commercial skills of professionals – in the audio-visual sector.

Duration: 1991–1995. EC contribution: ECU 200 million.

Non-nuclear energy R&D

Continues the work of the previous programme, JOULE, to promote the development of new energy models that are environmentally safe and economically viable, including energy saving options.
    Duration: 1991 to December 1994. EC contribution: ECU 155 million is likely to be available for project support. Project eligibility: Projects must be pre-competitive and preference is given to proposals involving collaboration with bodies in other member states.

RACE II (Research and Development in Advanced Communications Technologies for Europe)

This communications technologies programme will support research and development in advanced communications systems, implementation strategies and their applications within various commercial sectors. RACE is designed to contribute towards the introduction of Integrated Broadband Communications taking into account the Integrated Services Digital Network and national introduction strategies. It will concentrate on areas of work which require the participation of two or more organizations from the telecommunications sector.
    Duration: 1990–1994. EC contribution: ECU 489 million.

SAVE (Specific Actions for Vigorous Energy Efficiency)

Aims to improve energy efficiency by harmonizing technical standards, coordinating fiscal incentives and influencing consumer attitudes.

Duration: 1994–1995. EC contribution: decided annually – 1993 was ECU 6.5 million.

SPRINT (Strategic Programme for Innovation and Technology Transfer)

To strengthen the innovative capacity of European suppliers of goods and services. SPRINT promotes the use of new technologies throughout the Community's economy and the transfer of new technologies to SMEs.

Duration: 1989–1993. EC contribution: ECU 90 million.

SPRINT – TPF (Technology Performance Financing)

To facilitate the uptake of new technology by companies/SMEs. To improve the liquidity and strengthen the competitive position of European suppliers of new technology, many of which are also SMEs. It aims to stimulate the uptake of new technology in traditional industries by linking payment to the performance of the technology supplied.

TEDIS II (Trade Electronic Data Interchange System)

To coordinate the development of electronic data interchange (EDI) systems for trade, industry and administration, taking into account the specific needs of the users, including those of SMEs. The benefits of the programme are perceived to be a lowering of operating costs; the elimination of delays in transmission of quotations, contracts, invoices and data entry; and the elimination of errors in transcription.

EC contribution: ECU 25.4 million with an additional contribution expected from EFTA (European Free Trade Association) of approximately 14 per cent. Grant assistance: the programme provides organizational support to participants for the creation of EDI communities and shows

SMEs how to participate as EDI users. Funding of up to 50–100 per cent of project costs may be available.

Telematic systems

Concerned with research and development in the application of information technology and telecommunications. See details under the heading Telematics systems in Chapter 9.

Mastering of energy technologies

THERMIE has replaced the Community programmes on projects which demonstrate energy savings and technological developments in the hydrocarbon sector. The primary aim of the programme is to improve energy efficiency, the diversification and security of supply and the protection of the environment, by making use of economically justified technologies. It intends to promote the application of the results of energy R&D at a commercial scale and provide opportunities for European engineering industry by encouraging replications of the demonstration projects.

Duration: 1990–1995. EC contribution: ECU 700 million. Grant assistance: funds of up to 40 per cent of eligible costs may be available. Eligible costs may include the cost of the innovative part of the project, extra costs over a conventional installation or total project costs.

PETRA II (Action for the Training and Preparation of Young People for Adult Working Life)

PETRA promotes the expansion, improvement and diversification of vocational education and training opportunities. This programme seeks to ensure that young people receive at least one year's vocational training.

Duration 1992–1995. EC contribution: ECU 177.4 million.

CHAPTER 11

Selling to the Multinational Corporations

What has this to do with selling into the internal market? The multinationals in Europe are highly Europeanized, most of them, particularly US companies, run by nationals of the member states in which they are located. They are very responsive to European conditions and regulations, and world leaders in the areas of advanced management techniques, sometimes first developed in Europe, such as the practice of implementing quality and environmental standards to ISO specifications. They are influenced by European public procurement practices and, in turn, influence them, especially in the business of establishing relations with suppliers. They have been a potent force in marrying the best of European practices with world class techniques and, in turn, promoting them back to corporate headquarters and to sister companies across the world. Finally, they are huge purchasers of products and services, within the EC and EFTA, and throughout the rest of Europe.

Later in this chapter, the specifics of the contractual dealings with multinationals will be dealt with, including life-of-programme agreements and supplier verification procedures, but first it may be useful to discuss the general requirements which suppliers must meet before selling to MNCs, and supplier here means consultant, accountant, caterer, landscape gardener, waste remover, cleaner, as well as the so called 'vendor' or materials and components supplier. One will find the same conditions imposed upon the stationery supplier who stocks office cabinets on a JIT basis as those imposed upon the ship to stock, or ship to point of use, packaging supplier.

Perhaps the first and most all embracing characteristic of the current customer–supplier relationship in Europe is that it has become much closer, and one reason or consequence of this is that there are fewer suppliers for each component or service, one only being the preference. This presents prospects which have both challenges and opportunities, the latter being the great expansion in business as the customer asks for everything in the range to be supplied, the former the task of meeting such an increased requirement at the levels of service and quality required. The closer relationship means that, increasingly, the supplier is a part of the customer's system, and this is especially true in a KANBAN – 'sell one – make one' or JIT environment (KANBAN is a Japanese expression, while JIT is an acronym for 'just in time'), where the supplier will probably be linked via electronic data interchange (EDI) into the customer's selling mechanism. These are, of course, Japanese techniques copied by the western businesses, and now applied throughout the world. Many of the other techniques are American, or global, and much of the information technology is American, especially telecommunications and mainstream computer processing.

At the end of this chapter, there is a list of techniques employed by the MNC manufacturers. In the first instance, potential suppliers must be able to cope with such techniques, and there now follow details of the more important steps in dealing with a sophisticated customer after one has acquired the necessary techniques and reached the levels of sophistication required. We are not discussing tendering here, which is a different process, used for all responses to public procurement offers and private sector projects, such as construction. There may be no tender stage in becoming a supplier to an MNC, but there will be a critical negotiation stage in which the early contact may be as informal as a telephone call to the potential buyer. The three very formal steps, which follow that early informal stage, however, are vendor appraisal, supplier certification, and contract or agreement. Before looking in detail at these it may be helpful to summarize the situation.

The early informal contact may be either a very profitable experience or a commercial disaster. It will be the latter if the applicant has not properly understood what is meant by 'world class'. The applicant should be expert in the subject matter and be prepared to ship to stock, in zero defect, under an ISO 9000 system, and (perhaps) an environmental management system. He or she should also be prepared to communicate with the customer using EDI.

If all this is apparent to the prospective customer, the next potentially rewarding steps may take place. The first is vendor assessment, although in many cases outside of specialist industries, such as computers and pharmaceuticals, holding ISO 9000 certification will probably suffice, making separate vendor assessments unnecessary. The actual vendor assessment will be carried out under the second process mentioned, which is supplier certification and (perhaps) ship to stock procedure.

Most sophisticated buyers will have a manual available, which will be given to potential suppliers, showing them what they have to do to achieve supplier certification status. What follows now is based on the writer's knowledge of how the Japanese electronics company ALPS does this for its procurement in its European plants.

The initial preamble to the document includes the statement that the purpose of the procedure is to develop a good business partnership between ALPS and its suppliers 'by working together to reduce overall costs for both suppliers and ALPS, while maintaining high quality standards'. It also lists the following advantages to the supplier: increased business opportunities, clear supplier expectations, improved quality by planning for quality and documenting the plan, less scrap and fewer returns, thus reducing overall costs, and helping to make the supplier more competitive in the marketplace.

A key element in the procedure is the Approved Supplier Part, which is the status of the supplied part after going through the assessment procedures. This status can reflect a continual capability of meeting the quality requirements, a guarantee of being defect-free and consequently allowed into the ALPS processes without the need for incoming inspection, or the ranking achieved through the ALPS audits.

The contact procedure gives an interesting insight into the informality of the early stage and bears out what is written about contacts above. If as a result of preliminary discussions there is an intent to do business by both parties, a representative of the purchasing department provides all the necessary information to the supplier, including an uncontrolled copy (in the ISO 9000 sense) of the latest revision drawings and specifications for the part being sourced. A representative from the quality assurance department may also send a copy of the certification procedure to the supplier, so that he or she may understand the ALPS policy on supplier certification. The selection criteria are specified and these may include a demonstration pre-production run. If selection results, the supplier is added to the approved list.

The four measurement characteristics are:

- Production performance, measured in quality acceptance.
- Delivery performance, measured in number of stoppages due to supplier errors.
- Holding excess stock – documentation accuracy.
- Quality accuracy.

Key areas of focus during the audit of the supplier are: the quality management organization (viz. ISO 9000), drawings and specifications control, process and product specification control, material, storage, handling and record retention, control of purchased material, cost reduction and value analyses, the management of own suppliers, ship to stock status with other customers, and records of customer service. They also look for a training programme in quality control.

ISO 9000 is an ideal mechanism for helping to achieve the conditions demanded above; indeed, as already remarked, this is all that may be required for selling to companies less demanding than those in the electronics industry. To the demands listed above, increasingly in the years ahead, will be added those of environmental conformance.

In Appendix 1 Amdahl has kindly allowed the reproduction of both its life-of-programme agreement and the terms and conditions of the agreement. A quick glance at these here, however, reveals the following interesting demands. Suppliers have to achieve and maintain ISO 9000 approval. This is now common across multinational buyers and has become a primary requirement.

According to a supplied forecast, goods will not arrive more than two days in advance of forecast due date, and will never be late. Suppliers must indemnify and hold the customer harmless from any loss or liability arising out of happenings within the customer's premises. The supplier may be asked to allow inspections by the customer at the supplier premises, while acceptance will not take place until after final inspection at the customer's plant. The customer can change the specifications or methods of shipment at any time. The onus is on the supplier to comply with all laws and regulations. The supplier agrees to confidentiality concerning the customer's operations. This is probably the most difficult clause, as a supplier will want to use the success of selling to one company to open doors into others in a similar area and who will inevitably be competitors. The supplier cannot subcontract without permission from the customer, another difficult clause, except where the customer is flexible about subcontracting.

The paragraph about gifts is also very interesting, and a very welcome one also. The supplier shall not make or offer a gratuity or gift of any kind to customer employees or their families. The customer will interpret any such gratuity or gift as an improper attempt to influence the customer's employees. Here we are seeing the far reaching consequences of the spread of independent third part accreditation under systems such as ISO 9000 and, it is hoped, the end of the corruption of favouritism and closed groups.

We will now look at specific techniques employed by MNCs.

Advanced manufacturing technology (AMT)

Advanced manufacturing technology (AMT) applies to the whole environment of manufacturing, as distinct from some specific application of AMT, such as robotics or JIT. It describes the present state of a process which began with the industrial revolution, when the harnessing of energy allowed both machinery, and its automation, to replace people.

Selling to a company using AMT techniques will almost certainly oblige the seller to adopt these also, especially if the product is being supplied into inventory or to the production line. The steps towards AMT are mechanization in the first instance, automation of groups of machines, overall computer integrated manufacturing (CIM), and finally creating an environment, which goes beyond the factory, involving communications between customer and supplier.

AMT also involves production methods and production management systems, known as PMS. These include the MRP, Materials Requirements Planning, and Manufacturing Resource Planning systems. AMT involves the automation of machines themselves, as in robotics, the automation of their control through adding computer power to each machine, the controlling of clusters of machines and whole production lines in CIM, the use of sophisticated production management systems such as the MRP, mentioned above, or KANBAN, and the employment of such working interfaces with customers and suppliers as JIT, just in time delivery, and EDI, electronic data interchange.

Computer integrated manufacturing (CIM)

This environment will also have a profound effect on suppliers. CIM is often the environment pictured when people talk about the factory of the future, where discrete manufacturing is moving towards process or flow manufacturing. Some commentators see it as the integrated application of computer technology to manufacturing.

CIM is usually accomplished in three stages. The first is to simplify the process, and this usually means employing other AMT devices, such as IT, EDI, and the ISO 9000 quality management system. It may also mean using a system of production management such as MRP or KANBAN. The second step is to automate, perhaps using robots, and the third step will be to use computers to integrate all of the data and systems needed to control the whole manufacturing operation.

The MNCs are now moving towards round the clock operation, very small production lot sizes or batches, greatly reduced lead times between the suppliers of parts to the factory and the delivery from the factory to the customer, little or no human labour at the point of production, and, finally, a small factory, not a large one.

Just in time (JIT)

This has been called the supply of exactly the required items, at exactly the required quality, in exactly the required quantities, at exactly the right time, and it has a profound effect on suppliers.

JIT is the expression of two important emerging phenomena in the new trading environment – those of changing customer–supplier relationships and time compression, or reduced lead times. The change most in evidence is closer links between supplier and customer, expressed chiefly through JIT, where the supplier comes right into the factory to stock the production line, allowing for the elimination of stores and, even, incoming inspection.

As we saw above, the changing relationships also mean that the customer is dealing with fewer suppliers in each category, the present norm with world class manufacturers being to deal with one only in each. These new relationships, which require giving suppliers as much trust as one would an employee, are based on other developments in the new manufacturing environment, chiefly quality. One can only begin to consider allowing a supplier into one's factory to stock the production line when that supplier has a verifiable system of quality management, such as that demonstrated by ISO 9000. If the supplier tries to simulate real JIT by carrying hidden stocks, he will not be able to meet the other demand of his customer – a product manufactured at the lowest possible cost.

The aims of JIT are the elimination of waste, the reduction or elimination of inventories, and manufacture to the right specifications, and at the right time. JIT is also being made possible by EDI, electronic data interchange.

Electronic data interchange (EDI)

When everything else is in place, EDI follows naturally. If a supplier operating under a top quality management system and delivering daily, or overnight, in JIT tries to communicate with his customer via the ordinary mail for orders and invoices, it will become apparent very quickly that much more rapid means of communication are needed to do justice to this new working relationship.

EDI involves the elimination of paper for orders, deliveries, invoices and, in some cases now, even payments, and using computer to computer links instead. A very good example of EDI can now be seen in US and European supermarkets where the scanner at the checkout or 'till', is counting the number of products purchased and triggering off re-orders through the supermarket computer. In fact the supplier is receiving both orders and 'till forecasts' directly from retail customers over EDI.

One can only deal directly, computer to computer, with a few customers or suppliers, for reasons of logistics and interface standards, so third party operators called value added networks (VANs), offer to carry all the electronic trade messages over their own networks. These are covered in more detail in Chapter 23.

Related to EDI is electronic mail (E.Mail). Where EDI is for the formal or structured data representing the data of business transactions, such as orders, E.Mail is the electronic transmission of the kind of messages formerly sent by telephone, or communicated face to face, now dispatched by, and stored on, computers, for the receiver to attend to when convenient.

CHAPTER 12

Training Opportunities

The market for training in Europe, and indeed for training in world markets in EC matters, is incalculable. In fact the potential is such that in a number of areas it is virtually a supplier's market. The reasons will be made clear by the chapters of this book dealing with regulations, but a number of general comments may first be helpful.

Everywhere we are seeing less of the hardware element in a transaction and more of the related services, including training; even within products, such as hardware and software, the training elements are increasing. The development of the practice of outsourcing, discussed in Chapter 10, merely increases the emphasis on external training, although training by its very nature, like reading books or going to the movies, was more likely to come from the outside, because of the need to source imaginative new ideas and new methods of presentation.

Two major new factors have opened up the internal market, from inhouse practices and from beyond national borders, to training opportunities. First, the spirit of the market itself with its emphasis on the elimination of internal frontiers, and, second, the finalizing of the opening up of public procurement, especially through the services directive, which included training.

These two great motivating forces, which resulted essentially from the removal of barriers, came about at a time when several other forces were boosting the training market. The first, which was not European-driven was the continuing expansion of technology and its hunger for training material – witness the growth in technical writing and the proliferation of user manuals and online help routines. But the most recent EC-driven force has come from new regulations and standards, some derived directly from the EC, others such as ISO standards, boosted by it.

Chapters 14 to 21 deal in more detail with the main areas of regulations and standards – quality, environment, health and safety, product standards, but some aspects need to be singled out for a more detailed scrutiny. To study management standards and regulatory areas of training we can select two broad areas, which are voluntary in theory and mandatory in practice, and one compulsory area.

These two broad areas are quality and environment, covered by the two standards ISO 9000 and BS 7750 and in the case of the latter by the EC Eco-management scheme regulation as well. Both of these demand the training of staff if one is to achieve certification. These demands are for continuing training. These needs are also being boosted constantly by the demands of customers who impose the ISO 9000 requirements down upon their suppliers and also impose their own specific training demands, in whatever disciplines are being employed. Such are the demands of buyers in the two areas of quality and environment that one may safely assume that both the standards, and the training involved, are indeed mandatory as far as the market is concerned, if not legally required.

The compulsory area is that of health and safety regulations which are legally binding, and they include a legal requirement to train all staff. Apart from this compulsion, there are strong corporate and personal reasons why employers should train staff as the new legislation also makes staff responsible for their own safety if they are trained, thus sharing the burden of responsibility with management. All of this has given a tremendous boost to training in the health and safety area, which is almost unique in its dependence on legislation and good management practice.

The voluntary part of the new environmental management standard is only that part not covered by specific regulations affecting specific issues, such as air and water, or legal liability arising out of product liability and negligent processing. Indeed, with so many parts of the environmental management subject to regulations, and with training in all of its aspects demanded by the 'voluntary' parts, one may assume that training is now compulsory in all aspects of environmental management. If there was any doubt about this, the spectre of a non-compliance causing an accident within a large processing plant and its consequent liabilities should eliminate it.

There are two broad categories of business in training. The first might be called 'flesh and blood', which is the use of live lecturers giving training courses or workshops, while the second is publishing in all its forms, from books to multimedia products.

The first can be big business for those consultants who are well organized and who can command sufficiently high daily rates to employ teams of specialist lecturers. The business in turn is greatly enhanced if one gains access to large corporations who open up their different locations and divisions to the training programme. The prospects offered by MNCs are very similar to those on offer through the liberalization of public procurement, and a training course accepted by one local authority in France, for example, might become available to all.

The second category, the published package, requires either a powerful inhouse marketing mechanism or an arrangement with a publisher who is capable of placing business products onto the business market. These are few and far between, and are made up of perhaps six well-known names internationally. The business book market today has expanded to include training material, such as videos, movies, packs, workshops and multimedia.

One major technological development affecting the training market is the expansion of the training platform from the seminar and school room to the workstation. In the former the media were celluloid or video; in the latter the media are totally digitized, such as those on CD-ROM (compact disc read only memory). This is of profound importance, because it means that the former quality media, that is broadcast, which excluded the so called consumer video, including the 'home video', no longer have an advantage, while the consumer or 'semi-pro' is totally at ease with the CD and the PC. Indeed, the broadcast standard may be at a disadvantage. The monopoly of broadcast media on quality production at the workstation level has been broken; now only the quality of the ideas and their production in terms of cost, script and shooting, are the constraints facing the consumer or hobby artist. This is, of course, true only at the workstation level, where visual limitations still apply. Broadcast quality still prevails on wider fronts – from training room to living room. The workstation, however, has a huge potential for application-specific training, which by its nature is well accommodated by non-broadcast video.

The PC with CD-ROM data is expanding the training market by widening its application to the workstation and by allowing in more service providers. In addition, the training application functions of the PC and CD-ROM are being added to by the information function as the CD-ROM makes basic management information available over the same device that does the training. This is another example of how technology affects both applications and definitions. While information is updated weekly or monthly at the moment by CD-ROM, broadband and related technologies will shortly make it practical to have real time updated information online at the workstation. The areas of information being made available are marketing, legal, medical, environmental, financial and so on, as well as news.

As we noted in Chapter 8, publishers are now expanding their products not only to film and video, but to CD-ROM devices and to online videotext systems. They are faced in the short to medium-term with servicing two markets – the traditional seminar room, with its demand for conventional video, and the workstation with its combined training.

Meanwhile, technology is enabling the nature of training itself to change. It is now believed that only by empowering workers and giving them real insights into the workings of the whole organization will training be effective. In the European context, this is clearly seen in the way ISO 9000 training empowers staff with responsibilities for product quality and in the way staff are made responsible both for their own health and safety and for the environment. Indeed, as will be made clear in Chapter 18, in the health and safety regulations, training transfers legal responsibilities for safety from management to workers, or at least shares it with them.

CD-ROM also permits multimedia applications, including text, graphics, audio and full motion video, which are all stored on the one disk. Also being developed at the workstation level in Europe are simulated scenarios in an 'as needed' mode for the worker to simulate 'what if' situations and learn from the results. Case studies are also becoming popular as are customized inhouse applications. The instructor can be an outside consultant or well-known author, a retired expert or the company president.

CD-ROM, with its ability to house 250,000 pages on a single compact disc is now a publishing medium competing with printed books, microfilm and microfiche, and it can also be accessed online. A large number of European and international databases are now available on CD-ROM. Much of the kind of information on opportunities and regulations contained in this book is also amenable to the medium of CD-ROM.

While one may say that the potential for selling services into the internal market is very great, that for selling training services is enormous, if for no other reason than that every worker in Europe is now being trained for both mandatory legal reasons and in the drive for European excellence.

CHAPTER 13

Investing
in Europe

This chapter is aimed at potential investors outside Europe as the subject of partners within Europe has already been discussed. The method looked at here is that of making an investment, either in Europe or elsewhere, by finding a European partner or by setting up a company and hiring European staff.

The three common ways of investing in Europe, apart from buying real estate, are to start up a company, purchase a company, or invest in one. In all three cases, the usual approach is to staff the company with nationals; indeed, so confident are US owners in Europeans that US companies in Europe tend to have nationals in all jobs including that of chief executive officer (CEO). Two other ways of reaching the internal market are to sell through an agent or distributor and to license one's products, but neither of these are investing in Europe in the strict sense.

The poorer countries of Greece, Portugal, Spain and Ireland are attractive venues as are certain regions of the more wealthy countries, such as Wales and Scotland. Ireland's rather peripheral geographic position is somewhat offset by a modern telecommunications network and a very skilled and highly-educated English speaking workforce. Scotland and Wales can make similar claims. What these poorer regions offer, however, is a very sophisticated state support system which helps overseas companies who are in manufacturing and certain services, to set up in their territories. All are actively encouraging both EC and non-EC companies to invest by settling into local facilities. These agencies also provide grants and tax reliefs as incentives.

The best way of finding out what each country has to offer is to contact individual local embassies and ask the trade attachés to have the appropriate development agency forward material. Many of these agencies, such as Ireland's aggressive Industrial Development Authority (IDA), have overseas offices. This is certainly the best approach if one has decided on one country or is choosing between two. If, however, one wants to look across the whole of the EC or Europe, this is a different matter. In this instance, one may need the services of an international firm of consultants.

Arthur Andersen has an excellent set of publications describing how to invest in the European market. Amongst these are the following:

> *Building a Stake in Europe: Guidelines for US Investors in Real Estate*
> *Headquarters Locations in Europe*
> *The Arthur Andersen European Community Sourcebook*
> *Holding Companies in Europe*
> *How to Set up Business in Denmark*
> *A Guide to Investment in Germany*
> *Grants and Other Assistance in Ireland*
> *Irish International Financial Services Centre*
> *Doing Business in Italy*
> *Luxembourg Holding Companies*
> *Investment in Netherlands Real Estate*
> *Investing in Portugal*
> *A Guide to Business in Spain*
> *Establishing a Business in the UK*

The best way to obtain these is to apply to one's local Arthur Andersen office.

Apart from investing directly in a European company, one may find a European partner, either to work on a project within Europe or on a project overseas. The most likely reason for the first is to cooperate on a large public procurement project, probably in public works or supplies. As will be seen in the chapters on public procurement (Chapters 5–8), long before the opening up of the public procurement market across the internal market, there was already a tradition of buying certain categories of product outside the country of use, usually because that was the only way to obtain it, for instance computers and tele-communications.

Partnerships, however, can allow the European buyer to have the best of both worlds – to buy European and to have the possible technical superiority of the non-European partner. Any non-European company interested in helping a European partner obtain public procurement contracts should read the chapters on public procurement (Chapters 5–8), and then scan the daily list of tenders to see what typically is being advertised.

There are two other forms of cooperation with European partners for projects outside of Europe. One is using EC support, while the second is using support and opportunities provided by the World Bank and by 'outside of Europe' in this context we mean outside of the EC and EFTA, as projects in eastern Europe may also qualify for support.

The EC has a programme called 'International Scientific Coopera-tion'. This is to promote cooperation between laboratories in the European Community and third countries in Latin America, Asia and the Mediterranean region. The cooperation takes place within the framework of bilateral cooperation agreements which the Community has signed with the different countries. Those currently involved are:

Latin America:	Argentina, Bolivia, Brazil, Chili, Columbia, Costa Rica, Ecuador, El Salvador, Guatemala, Honduras, Mexico, Nicaragua, Panama, Peru, Uruguay and Venezuela.
Asia:	Saudi Arabia, Bahrain, Bangladesh, Brunei, China, United Arab Emirates, Philippines, India, Indo-nesia, Kuwait, Malaysia, Mongolia, Pakistan, Qatar, Singapore, Sri Lanka, Thailand and Yemen.
Mediterranean:	Israel and Yugoslavia.

The Community sponsors joint research projects and allocates grants to qualified scientists from third countries to visit European laboratories. Workshops to promote personal contacts and to prepare joint research projects are also supported. The areas concerned are medical research, biology, agriculture, environment, earth sciences, material sciences, physics, chemistry, mathematics, and engineering.

The European Bank for Reconstruction and Development (EBRD) funds developments in the countries of central and eastern Europe, and many contracts are available, from the Baltic to the Urals, funded by the EC's Phare and Tacis programmes.

The World Bank is owned by more than 155 countries and consists of the International Development Association (IDA), and the International Bank for Reconstruction and Development (IBRD). Its central purpose is to promote economic and social progress in developing nations. What The World Bank can mean for both EC and non-EC companies and consultants can be seen from a glance at the *Monthly Operation Summary* (MOS) of the International Business Opportunities Service (IBOS). The MOS reports on the status of every project in the World Bank's pipeline, from the point of identification of investment opportunities to project approval. There are about 800 project entries in each MOS issue.

While the European Bank also funds projects worldwide, it does much more in central and eastern Europe than the World Bank. The World Bank's projects will be found worldwide especially in what has been called the Third World. There can be opportunities for cooperation between EC and non-EC companies on projects funded from both of these sources, as well as those funded by the African Development Bank and the Asian Development Bank. To qualify for projects funded by either of the last two, the country of the applicant company must be a member of these banks. The point of view taken here is that of the contractor or consultant, not that of the company or government in the recipient country.

PART III

The Tighter Regulations

CHAPTER 14

European Standardization

The most important question for companies outside Europe is whether Europe is a land of opportunity or a closed market. Europe, in this case, is the EC, EFTA with eastern Europe joining in. The answer is that Europe is an open market, full of opportunities, if outsiders know what is going on in the standardization process. The chapters which follow deal with certification, compulsory standards, the CE Mark and certification, but here the general European standards situation will be reviewed.

The good news is that the standardization process, although given a huge impetus by Europe, is a worldwide one promoted and coordinated by such bodies as the International Organization for Standardization (ISO), with headquarters at Geneva and the International Electrotechnical Commission (IEC).

ISO is a worldwide organization, made up of national standards bodies from 94 countries. It promotes the development of standardization to facilitate international trade and to develop cooperation in the standardization process. It publishes international standards in all fields except electrical and electronic engineering, which are the responsibility of its sister body, IEC. ISO has thousands of experts in technical committees and works with governments, industry, and the scientific community.

The first fact then about European standards is that the most important of them are, in fact, international standards, available through ISO and the IEC and through 74 'member bodies' of ISO worldwide. Not all developing countries have member bodies, but 20 of them are known as 'correspondent members', who are also kept fully informed.

Within Europe the standards bodies are:

- The national standards bodies within each member state, such as BSI (UK), DIN (Germany), AFNOR (France), NSAI (Ireland).
- The national electrotechnical committees, such as BEC, (UK), DKE (Germany), ETCI (Ireland).
- CEN/CENELEC, the Joint Standards Institute on common matters, who provide the EC with standards.
- ETSI, the European Telecommunications Standards Institute.

The members of CEN are the national standards bodies of each EC and EFTA country; the members of CENELEC are the Electrotechnical Committees of each EC and EFTA country.

For countries inside Europe, the bodies to be aware of, and to influence, are CEN/CENELEC. Several eastern European countries and Turkey are now affiliate members. Most industries, through their associations, need to be represented on the CEN/CENELEC technical committees, as these are constantly creating new European standards which affect how they do business. The non-European countries have access to ISO/IEC. Both ISO/IEC and CEN/CENELEC closely mirror each other's activities, with the proviso that, at the time of writing, a number of European standards were leading the process, so that a European standard could be more advanced than an international standard at any one time. The member countries of CEN/CENELEC, and their standards bodies are, of course, also members of ISO/IEC. The affiliate members of CEN/CENELEC are those expected to become EC or EFTA members.

CEN/CENELEC do try to use international standards in creating European standards. It may not be so much a case of better European standards as more of them, as the internal market develops, but ISO and

IEC are working very closely with CEN/CENELEC. Duplication of effort is avoided, as ISO representatives attend CEN meetings, and CEN members attend ISO meetings. ISO/IEC may even be asked to develop work for CEN.

The first consideration therefore for any product directed at Europe is that it should meet with the requirements of an international standard where there is an international standard for the product accepted in Europe. Where there is a European standard, which may also have an international equivalent, the technical details will be obtained by referring to the EN document describing the 'European Norm' or European Standard. If the product is in a category covered by an EC directive, such as machinery, electrical, children's toys, building products, medical devices and gas appliances, all the requirements of the directive must be met. These will usually in turn be satisfied by meeting the requirements of individual product standards – there may be many components, each with a standard, with each overall product covered by a directive. Even a concrete block has components with at least three standards.

If the product does fall into a category covered by a directive, in one of the categories listed above, it now needs to carry a CE Mark to guarantee it free circulation within the EC (see Chapter 24 for more details of the CE Mark). To qualify for the CE Mark, all the components contained within the product will need to satisfy the requirements of relevant European standards.

For a number of reasons, the manufacturer may need to implement an ISO 9000 quality management system. If the product is covered by a directive, the directive may demand this. Many European standards bodies now insist on ISO 9000 before certifying some products to a product standard. Virtually all MNCs and sophisticated buyers, as well as public procurement buyers, are demanding ISO 9000 compliance.

The ISO 9000 system itself will have to be certified by a qualified certification agency, as may the standards which apply to each product in cases where the product is covered by directives. The word 'may' is deliberately used, and full details are given later in a discussion of the CE Mark in Chapter 24.

Even this will not be enough for those manufacturers insisting on carrying out vendor assessments and continuous checks on incoming components until such suppliers are qualified through performance to ship to stock.

At the time of writing, both the EC Eco-management and audit scheme regulation and BS 7750, the environmental management standard, were coming on stream. Even before their emergence, some companies were asking suppliers for demonstration of compliance with good environmental practice. All the signs are that this process will increase during the second half of the decade so that suppliers into Europe, and within it, will be increasingly asked to demonstrate compliance with either, or both, the environmental standard or the Eco-regulation.

As far as outsiders are concerned, therefore, both adherence to standards and certification by an EC or EC-accepted, which may be called an 'EC-notified', body are essential. Because of the demands, however, of both the CE Mark (for products covered by it) and the new consumer legislation, manufacturers outside Europe also need an authorized representative or retailer inside the EC prepared to take responsibility for product liability and product safety, in all instances, with or without the CE Mark.

Companies from countries within the EC can ignore the workings of CEN/CENELEC, except where they need to have technical representation, and depend instead on either, or both, their industry associations or local standards authority for information about European standards, with the proviso, of course, that from the point of view of marketing their end product they must always know what is going on. Companies from countries outside Europe need to keep in contact with strong local standards bodies, where such exist, or with ISO and the IEC.

ISO and IEC – general background notes

ISO, which was founded in 1947, came into being after about fifty years of electrical standardization – hence the separate IEC. ISO finally came into being to deal with general standards. It is now the largest standards organization in the world, with nearly 2,000 working groups, over 170 technical committees, and over 600 working and ad hoc groups, involving over 20,000 experts worldwide. It has published more than 8,000 ISO standards and it has national members from 94 countries.

Von Siemens probably began modern standards by asking the German PTB to standardize his dangerous new commercial product of electricity in the 1890s. The International Electrotechnical Commission was formed in 1906, and now has 42 national committees representing most of the world's electricity users. The IEC promotes international standardization in the fields of electrical and electronic engineering. It publishes standards, of which there are now over 3,000 and it has over 200 international committees.

Products covered by EC directives

Here is a list of products covered by EC directives. Anyone selling these within or into Europe needs all of the standards just discussed.

Product	EC directive	
Simple pressure vessels	87/404/EEC	1987
Toys (safety of)	88/378/EEC	1988
Building products	89/106/EEC	1988
Needing electromagnetic compatibility	89/336/EEC	1989
Machinery (safety of)	89/392/EEC	1989
Personal protective equipment	89/686/EEC	1989
Non-automatic weighing machines	90/384/EEC	1990
Implantable medical devices	90/385/EEC	1990
Gas appliances	90/396/EEC	1990
Telecommunication terminal equipment	91/263/EEC	1991

There are also a number of other devices covered by compulsory standards, which in turn carry national and EC regulations. These are all electrical devices, including plugs, babies' pushchairs, prams, soothers, the ignitability of furniture, the flammability of children's nightdresses, the ventilation of caravans, the breaking point of children's anorak cords (in case they catch in swings), and imitation sweets and candy.

CHAPTER 15

Products Needing Standards

The different countries of the EC have thousands of product standards. Some of the smaller countries may have hundreds, and where, formerly, they may not have had their own national standard for a specific product, such as paint say, they will have simply adopted the British, or French, or German standard for that product. Where the EC has adopted a harmonized standard for its member states these are called EN or European Standards. Each of these may have a correspondent national number in its own state – IS for Irish, BS for British, and so on.

Product standards range from building products to prams, from electronics to children's toys, and from electrical appliances to pharmaceuticals. Only a few standards are compulsory, and these are discussed in a moment, the rest are 'voluntary', which more and more means mandatory as far as the market is concerned, because one is no longer able to sell a product into the internal market if it does not conform to an EC or ISO standard.

In the buildings and construction areas, for example, there are standards for bricks, plaster, asphalt, wall ties, timber, roofing products, pipes, windows, doors, and furniture. Other typical product areas covered by standards are agricultural equipment, coal, coke, electrical, electronics, food and drink, gas cylinders, heating and ventilation, and hospital equipment. Other general areas of standards are household equipment, information processing systems, telecoms, motor vehicles, paper and stationary, plastics and rubber, plumbing, printing, safety, security, surface coatings, textiles, tools, and upholstery.

One of the main unification measures in the creation of the single market has been the harmonization of national standards. Up to the time of the movement towards the single European market, different national standards were a serious technical barrier to trade, although it must be said that CEN, the European Committee for Standardization, had done much pioneering work even before the beginnings of the formation of the Community towards making standards uniform across Europe. Europe is much more advanced now in this respect than the US and Canada, despite the US–Canada Free Trade Agreement, and standards can be a barrier to trade even within Canada itself, where different provinces may use different standards. A prairie province has been known to purchase for public works and supplies from across the border in the US, rather than from Ontario or Quebec, and to use its provincial standards to support this less than patriotic activity. Ironically now, Europe, despite its different languages and cultural diversity, is on its way to becoming a real single market on the basis of harmonized standards, and the elimination of standards being used as technical barriers to trade, against which the harmonization and solidarity promised by the US–Canada Free Trade Agreement may not compare.

The specifications for each product are published by the standards authorities of each country. You will first find your standard by reference to the national standards catalogue, then purchase the exact standard document for your selected product, and this will usually have a contents of ten pages or less, in general describing the following:

- The components which go into making the product.
- The steps in the manufacturing process.
- The values, dimensions, or other relevant attributes.

This is extremely important as buyers, particularly in MNCs and public bodies, will specify the standard, and the standard, often coming complete with drawings, is as good a specification as one supplied by the prospective customer. All EC countries have agencies for testing products, and these will be the accredited bodies. This is discussed in more detail in Chapter 24.

Most of these product standards are voluntary, in the sense that they are not covered by legislation, but, being commercial standards, while not compulsory under law, they are mandatory in as much as they are demanded by buyers. Europe as elsewhere continues to have a free and unrestricted market for non-standard products from gift items to junk, but this scene is changing as the regulatory environment widens. The only category of product which would seem to be immune from standards and legislation in the long-term is that of the cultural and artistic production, whether that is an oil painting, or the content of a book or television script. Nothing else appears to be safe. If product standards do not come to bear on a device, environment standards may. Meanwhile, side by side with increasing legislation, the trend towards virtually mandatory standards set by industry and large buyers continues.

While the technical barriers to trade have come down across the internal market through the harmonization of product standards, this process has set up severe technical barriers to trade between the European countries, EFTA included, and those Third World countries which cannot either produce to those standards or secure reputable certification, or who face having to send their output to a European testing agency. Harmonization with European standards is, to these countries, like the rebuilding of the Berlin Wall.

In the case of specialized international industries, such as airlines, aerospace, automotive, nuclear, pharmaceutical, and medical products, the EC is no different to the rest of the developed world, where many US-led standards apply – indeed it would not be in Europe's interests to exclude itself from US or Japanese technology in such areas by trying to set up a European standard, particularly where all or most of a technology is imported. Nor would European companies want to standardize themselves out of export markets. Indeed, what has given a further impetus to the EC standards process is the increasing regulatory nature of US standards, particularly in food and drugs and the environment.

Most of these specialized international industries, such as airlines, are of course also regulated and certified through national government departments, such as transportation, and healthcare, while medical products are regulated and 'registered' worldwide through departments of health. The most competitive factor for a healthcare company in

Europe will be to have patented products registered by the national departments of health in each country.

Products and processes needing certification

The two categories of demand for the certification of products and processes are market and legislative. We will begin with the market demands.

In a large number of cases, one can manufacture a product to a standard in Europe and operate a system of self-certification, simply stating that one's product conforms to BSI or DIN or EN standard as the case may be. In certain specific cases, such as the manufacture of concrete for major structures, owners, main contractors, and local authorities will demand evidence that the product has been daily tested by an independent testing agency. The motivation for the manufacturer to submit to testing should be as much legal protection in the event of a defective product as market demand. In cases where there is no demand for continuous demonstration of product compliance, two other devices may help to ensure such compliance. The first is the employment of the ISO 9000 quality management standard, see Chapter 17, and the second is the employment by sophisticated buyers of vendor assessments in which samples will be taken of product compliance. ISO 9000 compliance assumes that all product and component standards are being met. In the less demanding European industries ISO 9000 may be sufficient to assure the buyer of product conformance; in the more demanding, the buyer will also demand a vendor assessment. These assessments have, however, been drastically reduced in number and scope with the advent of ISO 9000. For information on a typical vendor assessment see the details of the ALPS method in Chapter 11.

Compulsory standards

A compulsory standard is a standard backed by legislation in the country where the standard applies, the legislation normally being manifested in the form of a statutory instrument or act of parliament to make adherence to the standard law. Where there is such a compulsory standard, it becomes a punishable offence to sell a product which does not conform to that related compulsory standard. Worse than the fine may be the fact that the European media is very fond of publishing news of the infringement of such standards and the names of the transgressing companies. And when one looks at the list of product areas one sees why. Typical consumer and product areas covered by compulsory standards are:

- Flammability of children's nightdresses.
- Toxicity and cellulosic content of children's toys.
- Ventilation of caravans and mobile homes.
- Safety of perambulators and pushchairs.
- Requirements for smoulder and flame resistant upholstery.
- Babies' soothers.
- Safety requirements for children's cots.
- Toxicity of pencils and graphic instruments.
- Rewirable 13 amp plugs.
- Safety of electrical equipment.
- Safety of workplace equipment.
- Anorak hood cords (covering the strength of hood cords in the anoraks of children under ten to prevent strangulation on swings and other apparatus).

In addition a number of products will be banned, such as erasers and other devices which may be manufactured to look, smell and taste like candy or sweets.

For all the member states, there are a number of additional legal requirements set out in standards, in such areas as electrical devices, telecoms, electronic emissions, radiation and so on. For example, under the EC 'Low Voltage Directive' we find the following:

- Safety of Household and Similar Electrical Appliances.
- Safety requirements for mains operated electronic and related apparatus for household and general use.
- Safety of electrically energized office machinery.
- Safety of data processing equipment.
- Lighting chains for Christmas and similar decorative purposes for indoor use.
- Safety of information technology equipment including electrical business equipment.

The CE Mark

This mark, placed upon a product, denotes that the product conforms to the requirements of all of the applicable EC directives and that testing has taken place in accordance with rules laid down in the directives. Examples of products covered by such directives are:

- Electrical.
- Machinery (safety).
- Construction.
- Telecom.
- Medical.
- Personal protective equipment.
- Toys.

The CE Mark denotes that the product conforms to essential requirements and is a 'passport' to European markets. It is not, however, an indication of quality. There is more about the CE Mark in Chapter 24.

Quality management systems standards

A revolutionary new development in Europe and throughout the world has been the use and acceptance of management systems standards. The best known of these up to now has been ISO 9000, European norm number EN 29000, the standard for quality management systems, and even this at the time of writing was showing signs of being moved into second place to the new environmental management standard. Both of these important standards have separate chapters devoted to them (see Chapters 17 and 19), but for our purposes here it is sufficient to point out how these management standards are being used in Europe.

Generally speaking the quality and environment management standards allow companies to demonstrate that they conform to all the product and process standards and regulations relating to the issues involved, and that they control their management and that of the whole system of production or service. In either case, standards accreditation is achieved only through independent third party inspections, which will be dealt with in Chapter 24, Testing and Certification. As already noted, this is not a guarantee that all vendor assessments will be waived, but they will, in many industries, either be reduced or eliminated, particularly in the more sophisticated activities, such as electronics, which form partnerships with their suppliers.

The four broad areas of management standards, covered by inspections, some of which are compulsory, are manufacturing quality, service quality, health and safety, and environmental standards. By 1994–95 the situation should be as follows. ISO 9000 will be a minimum requirement. By 1993, it had become a minimum requirement for selling to a European-based MNC, and into public procurement; indeed a US company in Europe was likely to be demanding it from suppliers even before its parent had achieved it at home. This gave rise to the fascinating business of standards authorities in the EC getting export business by certifying US companies in the US. The EC Eco-scheme regulation will be in the second year of its four year voluntary trial, as will its supporting environmental management standard BS 7750 (see Chapter 19), and an equivalent ISO standard, a green version of ISO 9000, or an expanded ISO 9000, will be widely in use, and increasingly demanded by buyers. The health and safety regulations (see Chapter 18), compulsory since 1989, and added to substantially in 1993, will be controlled under BS 7750 or its ISO equivalent.

The ISO 9000 services standard will be used widely by service and distribution companies to maintain or obtain market advantage. Service companies will have become aware of the similarities between the ISO 9000 services standard and the environment standards and will have implemented systems to demonstrate both. As ISO 9000 is intimately concerned with products as far as manufacturers are concerned, it is obvious that certification to ISO 9000 requires conformance to whatever standards apply to the products in question, such as type, safety, and compatibility, but what has actually happened is that certification agencies are demanding ISO 9000 as a pre-condition to type approving products. This process has been accelerated by the emergence of the CE Mark.

The CE Mark, as we saw, relates to the meeting of compulsory directives. To help meet the demands of these directives one uses European Standards (ENs), which are also published as national standards within each country. Each national government establishes the testing and certification systems and notifies the European Commission of the names of the testing and certification bodies. These are known as 'Notified Bodies'.

Here, for example, are the directives and demands for just one product – power supplies.

European Community Directives for Power Supplies

The directives are as follows:

- The CE Mark.
- The EMC [electromagnetic compatibility] Directive (89/336/ EEC).
- The Low Voltage Directive (73/23/EEC).
- The Telecommunications Terminal Equipment Directive (91/ 263/EEC).

One of the major achievements of the EC has been to harmonize standards across the Community, so that technical barriers to trade are removed and a real single market is created. Writing a directive is one thing, but to make it work or implement it, standards must be created. These are called the 'European Norms' and are identified by an 'EN' number, for example 'EN 55022'. Each national member state also uses these EN standards as equivalents to national standards, so that, for example, BS in the UK will have a BS/EN equivalent. This allows the member states to create national legal instruments where necessary to make some standards compulsory, for example, statutory instruments to implement safety standards for electrical appliances.

We see how complex all of this can be when we look more closely at just one of these directives, the EMC Directive (89/336/EEC). This came into force on 1 January 1992 and became law throughout most of the Community in 1993. It says that 'a product shall not cause interference with other equipment nor suffer from interference from other equipment in normal use'. This is a complex directive, which could take a full chapter to explain. There are seven separate standards associated with it for power supplies alone.

The Low Voltage Directive is also interesting and relates to all electrical devices. This compulsory directive states:

> The Member States shall take all appropriate measures to ensure that electrical equipment may be placed on the market only if, having been constructed in accordance with good engineering practice in safety matters in force in the Community, it does not

endanger the safety of persons, domestic animals or property when properly installed and maintained and used in applications for which it was made.

Quality approvals

These directives also require the demonstration of continued compliance throughout the period of manufacture. Certification of the manufacturing facility can be obtained through:

- ISO 9001, EN 29001.
- BABT 340.
- AQAP 4.

CHAPTER 16

Product Liability and Consumer Protection

Since the emergence of an EC directive on product liability in July 1985, member states have introduced product liability legislation with serious implications for manufacturers and distributors. The legislation relates to products only, not to service, and liability can be incurred by the producer for damages wholly or partly caused by a defect in a product, irrespective of whether the manufacturer was negligent. The damages may be in the form of personal injury or to property.

This stringent new legislation puts the position of the manufacturer *vis à vis* the end user or consumer into the same position as the world class supplier servicing a world class manufacturer in zero defect, shipping to the point of use on the production line. It reinforces the movement towards total quality control and the use of quality management systems to ensure total quality. It brings management standards under the scrutiny of both company lawyers and insurance companies. The state of corporate health is now also determined by the condition of its management standards.

Product liability extends to private consumers only and not to the actions of companies supplying each other, nor to an individual who obtains the product as part of his or her business. The concept of product under the legislation does not extend to primary agricultural products and other foodstuffs, such as unprocessed game. It means other movables including components.

Those potentially liable are manufacturers, their suppliers, including suppliers of both components and raw materials, and certain other persons who may put their own brand on a product. Of particular interest to non-EC manufacturers is that it also includes an importer of products from outside the EC, for example, Japanese or US products. It can even extend to retailers. The supplier, or retailer, cannot hide behind unnamed manufacturers and will be made liable in the event of not identifying the source. There is protection against frivolous claims and the onus on the injured person to prove the injury.

It would appear that the fundamental issue in product liability, for a claim to be possible, is a breach of safety. In the case of products which are inherently dangerous, labelling, advertising and, in certain cases, the issue of instructions and user manuals become all important. Anyone interested in this area should pay careful attention to the paragraphs on the safe use of products in Chapters 19 and 21.

The legislation also provides a defence for producers, and the grounds for exoneration from liability. Amongst these are those defects that arise after the product went into circulation, or that, because of the current state of technology, the defect could not have been known about at the time, or that the overall design of the product causes defects in the component or raw material in question. There is even an exception where 'compliance by the product with any requirement imposed by or under any enactment or any requirements of the law of the European Communities', which appears to be an extraordinary situation where having to conform to EC law, say a directive on telecoms, makes the product defective. Finally, the producer is not liable if he did not put the product into circulation, even though he made it. Products exchanged as private transactions also appear to be exempt – that is, not made for commercial purposes.

This strict new product liability comes after two other European protective measures for consumers, both covered by national and EC regulations. The first is consumer information, the second consumer rights. Consumer information legislation forbids false or misleading information about goods and services, including their prices, and extends to advertisements, claims by manufacturers and distributors, catalogues, pictures on packages, and even the oral claims of salespersons. Rather than conferring rights on the consumer, it brings criminal law to bear on the maker of the claims, imposing obligations of honesty and truth. The specific piece of EC legislation is the European Communities (Misleading Advertising Regulations) 1988.

The main areas where the consumer information legislation applies is to the description of products, and the offences are either to apply a false description to goods, or to sell or possess for sale goods to which a false description has been applied. This can make both manufacturers and retailers liable.

Description can be true or false relating to numbers, quantities, capacity, weight, place of origin, mode of manufacture, packages content, patents, fitness for purpose, conformity to standards, identity of supplier, standing or competence of manufacturer, contents of books, or as to their authors, or the contents of movies or recordings. This means that any false statement could make the producer liable. It may be a misleading picture rather than an explicitly false statement, for instance, a picture of a country different to that of origin.

Services also come under the scrutiny of consumer legislation. The statements which must not be misleading are those relating to the nature, effect or fitness for purpose of the service, and the time, place, manner or person by which the service is provided. The businesses to which these could apply range over hotels, travel agents, hairdressers, dry cleaners, accountants, lawyers, doctors and so on. The misleading information has to be of a material nature, relating to false or misleading indications given knowingly or recklessly. The last is not likely if the person making it believes it to be true. If, for instance, a careless statement about a future holiday resort was believed to be true at the time it was made, subsequent changes to the facts will not constitute recklessness.

One has to be very careful now in advertising to scrutinize such statements as 'no job too large or small', 'twenty-four hours a day service', 'untouched by human hand', 'home-made', 'solid gold', 'rain-proof', 'all mechanics fully qualified', and so on.

The correct price must be clearly displayed, and this includes extras such as installation or service charges, and should inhibit the use of top of the range models to give the impression that cheaper models have similar attributes. VAT must be included in displayed prices. 'Free gifts' accompanying the product cannot be recouped in a raised product price.

Even false claims of price reductions where a previous price is crossed through are forbidden. The use of recommended prices is strictly controlled.

Owners of multiple stores must take care that price reductions apply to every unit in a chain across a country.

Advertising agencies have to be careful not to knowingly publish advertisements which contain false or misleading information, and, in particular, not to become involved in designing campaigns and specific advertisements which use such information, as they also become liable. This also applies to certain publishers, such as newspapers, and to auctioneers. Editorial matter, not paid for by an advertiser, is excluded.

Apart from descriptions, other general requirements which apply under product liability are that the products must be of merchantable quality and be reasonably fit for the particular purpose for which the buyer intends them. The first of these is usually simply established – either the product does or does not work, but it is very difficult to establish in more complex cases of qualitative judgement. The second is also established where the product does not work in the intended application made clear at the time of purchase.

Product liability is given very specific significance in a number of areas. One of these is in the regulations which implement the European Directive on Food Labelling (79/112/EEC). These were last updated in 1992 and their purpose is to harmonize national legislation to achieve the free movement of foodstuffs throughout the internal market and to inform consumers of the minimum legal requirements.

In addition to the above regulations, specific and separate regulations also apply to other foodstuffs, such as:

- European Communities (Marketing Standards for Eggs) Regulations 1992.
- Food Standards (Certain Sugars) European Communities Regulations 1975.
- Food Standards (Honey) European Communities Regulations 1976.
- Commission Regulations EEC No 997/79 (wine and grape must) European Communities (Dehydrated Preserved Milks) Regulations 1980.

Returning to the directive on food labelling, the general requirements are that the labelling be clear, legible and indelible, in the language understood by the consumer, not obscured by pictorial or written matter and not be misleading. The regulation is quite specific about what should and what should not be in the information provided, and only the information which casts more light on the direction of consumer legislation in the EC is discussed here. Food manufacturers should read the regulation and apply it rigorously. Specifically excluded are claims for effects of properties which the product does not possess, and claims for special characteristics when all products of that class contain those characteristics. The labelling must not attribute to any foodstuff the property of preventing, treating or curing a human disease.

Amongst the key attributes which must be included are lists of ingredients, minimum durability (with exemptions), and, for perishables, use by date, and of interest to non-EC processors, the name and address of the manufacturer, packer, or seller established within the EC. This last is defined as the full postal address at which the consumer can contact a responsible authority in writing; a telephone number is not sufficient.

During 1992 the food labelling regulations also came into force for the catering trade, and where the product is not pre-packaged, the information must be contained on trade documents. The external packaging for the consignment must carry the name of the food, the date of minimum durability and a name and address of manufacturer, packer or seller in the EC.

Within each member state there is a certain leeway for authorities to amend and vary the food labelling regulations, so exporters from non-EC countries need to check with each contact in the specific market, distributor or other, to establish the exact nature of the regulation in that territory.

At the time of writing, another set of regulations was emerging which also affect the labelling and packaging of products. This is in the area of environmental packaging and labelling (see Chapter 20, Packaging and the Environment).

Misleading advertising can run the whole gamut from exaggerated claims to pure fraud. High on the list for the latter over the past twenty years in Europe were the activities of US pyramid selling companies, banned at home and now finally legislated out of Europe, but still operating in some of the poorer and less sophisticated regions under other guises, such as using token products, but still selling distributorships. These are now illegal under various pyramid selling acts. Also high on the list of complaints about misleading advertising has been the selling of timeshares. The UK Director General for Fair Trading made an important contribution to the reduction and elimination of this problem by recommending a number of requirements, included the submission of detailed prospectuses, a fourteen day cooling off period after the hard sell, the possibility of withdrawal and protection of deposits paid.

Other major areas of complaint have been financial leasing, the cost of loans and other financial packages, particularly in relation to buying automobiles and package holidays. Prices themselves are also a major cause of complaint.

Safety, however, continues to be a most important area and manufacturers should note the comments in Chapters 14 and 15 that a number of products are covered by legally compulsory standards, so that for those products such standards and their accompanying statutory instruments in the form of regulations are a minimum requirement.

Each member state has a consumer affairs or complaints department, which comes under a government department, such as commerce or industry. These are open to the consumer and provide free services. More importantly for the manufacturers, they also have powers of inspection and prosecution.

From all of this it is clear that the separate chapters on product standards, ISO 9000, the Eco-scheme regulation, and certification have considerable relevance to product liability. Above all BS 7750, the environmental management standard, provides the solution. Chapter 17 provides details of the ISO 9000 standard and Chapter 19 details of the environment standard. BS 7750 covers the environmental issues, the health and safety of employees, public safety and product use.

Product use or usability is becoming a major new area of liability for manufacturers. Perhaps the best way to illustrate this is through that most ubiquitous of products, software, and this is done in Chapter 21. As this subject is covered in much more detail there, all that will be said here is that while the health and safety regulations are directed at users, where they apply to end products, such as medical, electrical, software, those same products will be key environmental issues for their manufacturers, as product use is as relevant to the environment as emissions, effluent discharges and toxic waste, especially when their potential customers are bound by law not to use these products if they do not conform to regulations.

CHAPTER 17

ISO 9000

ISO 9000 has swept the world, starting in Europe where the European Community accepted it as the harmonized quality management standard for the Internal Market. Its official EN, European Norm, number is EN 29000. Being accredited to ISO 9000 is now essential for selling within and into the EC, or for selling to any MNC or sophisticated buyer in the world. It is also essential for selling into the EC public procurement market. Here we have just one chapter on this subject, but it is so important that readers new to the standard, or whose companies have not yet embarked upon it, should consult *ISO 9000*, second edition, by this author, and also published by Gower.

In 1987 ISO published the first five international standards on quality assurance, known as the ISO 9000 Standards. In their announcements at the time, they described the new standards as 'the refinement of all the most practical and generally applicable principles of quality systems'

and 'the culmination of agreement between the world's most advanced
authorities of these standards as the basis of a new era of quality
management'.

The 1987 edition of the generic ISO 9000 standard, in the document
bearing that number, had a clear mission of quality in the sense of
satisfying customer commitments, in particular, in delivering what was
promised or specified. The latest version to appear, however, is much
broader in its intended scope, and even messianic by comparison.
Indeed, if it is read by an experienced implementor of the environmental
management standard, it has a startling resemblance to it. It is almost as
if the ISO authors were preparing to expand ISO 9000 from quality to
embrace also the management of the environment. It lists five
'stakeholders', or vested interest groups, of which the customer is only
one and, together with owners and suppliers, names employers and
society. It specifically mentions workplace health and safety, the
protection of the environment, conservation of energy and natural
resources, and even security. All of these are the main requirements of
the new international environmental management standard, the first
model of which is BS 7750.

The authors state:

> Recognizing that the ISO 9000 series of International Standards
> provides a widely-used approach for management systems that can
> meet requirements for quality, these management principles can be
> useful for other concerns of society.

It claims that technical specifications can be developed for these
other areas, such as environment and health and safety, along similar
lines.

While it contains these aspirations, it does not provide for them to be
met. One can conclude only that ISO intends to repeat with BS 7750
what it did with BS 5750 – that is adopt it as a model, for at the time of
writing only the BSI BS 7750 standard was available for meeting such
aspirations, for ISO 9000 on its own cannot accommodate an entire
environmental management system, as there is more in the latter than
the former. At the time of writing, ISO still had not announced its
intentions with an ISO 9000-type environment management standard,
although news of such a move appeared to be imminent.

As it stands, the ISO 9000 standard document is devoted to
discussions on quality, quality system requirements and product
requirements. It makes the point that ISO 9000 standards are separate

from, but complement, product standards, and tells us that there are only four generic product categories, and that these are hardware, software, processed materials, and services.

The three main models of ISO 9000 are: ISO 9001, ISO 9002, and ISO 9003.

ISO 9001 is for those companies that need to assure their customers that conformity to specified needs is assured throughout the whole cycle from design through to service. This applies particularly where there is a contract specifically requiring design and where product requirements are stated in performance terms (speed, capacity, integrity). This is the fullest or most complete standard involving all the quality system elements detailed in ISO 9000 at their most stringent.

ISO 9002 is for those situations where one has an established design or specification, in other words most manufacturers who respond to a specification. Here all one has to demonstrate is capabilities in production and installation. It is less stringent than ISO 9001.

ISO 9003 is for demonstration of capabilities for inspection and test, where the product is supplied. About half of the elements of ISO 9000 are required here and an even lower level of stringency than for ISO 9002.

One can see from the foregoing that ISO 9000 in its original conception is seen as a system for quality management and quality assurance standards for the manufacturing environment. It provides the essential information needed to take management policy or quality assurance and converting it into action. It allows degrees of demonstration within the manufacturing environment and the production of evidence or proof that a buyer may require that the quality system is adequate and that the product conforms to the specified requirements, whatever they may be.

It applies to all manufacturing situations from full design, through manufacture to a supplied specification, installation and service, to final inspection and test centres and laboratories. It has enormous implications for manufacturing globally and particularly for manufacturers wanting to reach markets in the EC. As we saw in the chapters on public procurement and the MNCs, it also has profound implications for the relationships between manufacturers with both their customers and suppliers.

It is by no means just a regulatory mechanism, for it has a number of very specific advantages for the manufacturer apart from achieving the status and certification involved. Among these we could list the following:

- Improvements in production, productivity, housekeeping, quality of management, and quality of work.
- Reduction of waste, reruns, scrap.
- Improved order.
- Improved staff communications/morale.
- Improved customer/vendor relations.

There are two broad elements to ISO 9000. First any company can implement a quality management control system, based on the ISO 9000 standard, and simply state that it has implemented an ISO 9000 system, the proof of which is its own business. The second element is certification. Most buyers who care about ISO 9000 will demand proof of the reality of the ISO 9000 system through certification from a qualified and independent third party accreditation agency. This process is covered in more detail in Chapter 24.

Implementing the system itself is a matter of following the demands of the standard, particularly in ensuring that the specified requirements are adhered to, such as a formal policy, documented procedures, controls, rules for non-conformance, audits, reviews, and, in particular, control of both documentation and its amendments. One area contributing to the epidemic-like spread of ISO 9000 has been the demand that one's suppliers must also conform to the demands of the standard, and it is this more than anything else that has ensured worldwide compliance.

The standard is currently generating a new momentum as its services version begins to spread also. Simply known as the 'ISO 9000 Services Standard', its official title is 'ISO 9004 Part 2, Quality Management and Quality System Elements – Guidelines for Services'. This ISO 9004 standard is a whole family of guidelines, open-ended and, to an extent, exploratory, and it is the first attempt at quantifying what hitherto were regarded as sacrosanct qualitative issues in the service sector.

The standard applies to every service operation, but it lists the following: hospitality, communications, health, maintenance, utilities, general trade, financial, professional, administration, consultancy, technical services, purchasing, R&D. What are actually controlled are the service, which has characteristics observable to a customer and subject to customer evaluation, and the processes, through which the service is delivered to the user, but which may be invisible or not seen by the customer.

This rather difficult subject is covered in depth in *ISO 9000*, second edition, published by Gower, where the reader will also find a sample system, which is in fact used by ICL to demonstrate conformance to the requirements of ISO 9000 for a service company. Here, however, are some of the characteristics of a service, which are possible requirements which may be specified to measurable levels and controlled.

- The facilities including capacity, personnel and materials.
- Waiting, process and delivery times.
- Hygiene, safety, reliability, security.
- Responsiveness, accessibility, courtesy, comfort, aesthetics, competence, dependability, accuracy, completeness, state of the art, credibility and effective communication.

At the time of writing, there were actually more than thirty standards in the ISO 9000 series and in the related 10,000 series covering the auditing of ISO 9000 systems, and still more in the 45,000 series associated with certification.

Several new specific standards had emerged, in particular for software, process industries, dependability of management, services, processed materials, quality plans, and configuration of management. The software standard is most interesting for the implications it raises for a number of standards in the new highly-regulated Europe. There are a number of significant points to be made about this standard, which cast light upon the relationship of management standards with the regulatory environment, and they have been covered in the previous chapter.

The specific ISO 9000 standard for managing software development companies is ISO 9000–3, which demonstrates the managing of a quality system to control the production of software, and within that control system we have a detailed standard, ISO 9241, running to hundreds of pages, on how to write software. At the time of writing the only compulsory part of this standard was that portion relating to the visual display terminal (VDT) regulation, but software ergonomics were already being considered as an EC directive, as it is so ubiquitous and so many important and critical operations depend on good, ergonomically usable software.

This means that, at the very least, ISO 9241 is a code of practice, and it is not realistic that one should implement an ISO 9000 system, or an environmental management system, or a health and safety system, without adopting the standard which defines the code of practice. Placed alongside product and process standards in manufacturing, ISO 9241 becomes to ISO 9000–3 what the product and process standards are to ISO 9001 and ISO 9002. You cannot have one without the other.

This will be made even more difficult when read against Chapter 19, Environmental Management Standards, Chapter 16, Product Liability and Consumer Protection, and Chapter 21, General Legal Liability, and one realizes that software is used in many critical online processing situations and demands control also under the environment standard. To summarize, if you wish to implement ISO 9000–3 for your software, first make sure that you are already conforming to the VDT Regulation, then adopt ISO 9241 and finally ISO 9000–3. As we shall see shortly, a very interesting point here is that BS 7750 is already striding into new ground beyond ISO 9000 and anticipates all of this. To implement a BS 7750 system properly, a software manufacturer would have to implement both the VDT Regulation, that is cater for it in its products, and implement ISO 9241.

CHAPTER 18

The Health
and Safety
Regulations

While other standards discussed are for the most part voluntary, that is they may be mandatory for commercial purposes but are not covered by compulsory legislation, the EC health and safety regulations are legally compulsory. Many of them have been in force since 1989, but they were substantially updated by new 1993 directives. These regulations have implications for manufacturers in two main ways, which are as health and safety issues for those with staff in Europe, and, for certain products, as environmental issues for those selling into Europe. The word 'environmental' is used in the widest sense here, also covering public safety and product safety.

First, some comments on the relationships of environment, health and safety and quality. BS 7750 defines 'environment' to include the human and other 'living systems' within the surroundings and conditions in which the environment operates. It also asks that the environmental policy be consistent with the occupational health and safety policy. We saw in the last chapter that ISO 9000 was expanding to embrace worker health and safety. This in itself would be enough to warrant inclusion of health and safety under environment, but there is another good reason, which is that while much of the environmental demand is still voluntary, all of the relevant health and safety regulations are now mandatory and made legal under acts of parliament. The legislation also demands controls, and the environment standard and its control is the ideal vehicle for the incorporation of the health and safety demands and for the satisfaction of health and safety inspectors.

The commonest confusion is in the close relationship between health and safety and environment for certain products, which at times causes problems in differentiating the two. Packaging legislation comes into both areas, as do dangerous chemicals. A computer or software manufacturer will find VDUs are a health issue with internal staff, but an environmental issue with customers.

It helps to distinguish health and safety from both quality and environmental standards, although all three will shortly be integrated. You can produce a quality product in a manner inimical to both staff and the environment; you can also produce it in a safe and clean manner. Some health and safety issues go beyond the factory and become environmental matters – disposal of dangerous chemicals, toxic waste, emissions, for example, but taken in their narrowest sense the health and safety directives and regulations apply to workers and visitors to the workplace.

The scope of the regulations is quite wide. Before the 1993 additions there were already regulations in some specific formats and under an umbrella Framework directive. The 1993 directives made the legislation much more specific. The original 1989 EC 'Framework' regulation set the scene for what became a Safety, Health and Welfare at Work act in member states. This existing piece of legislation still stands, but is modified or given more substance by the specific new directives. Even before the 1989 legislation, there was a large amount of existing legislation. In the EC, for example, there are 32 regulations based on pre-Single European Act EC directives with health and safety implications.

Twenty of these relate to the classification, packaging, labelling, marketing and use of dangerous substances and preparations. Some of the new directives now update these. Three regulations fall under the infamous 'Seveso Directives' and relate to emergency planning at chemical plants. These arose from the Italian Seveso disaster. A number relate to the certification of electrical equipment, while one deals with safety signs at work. Four have to do with chemical, physical and biological agents at work.

Returning to the Framework directive and its member state equivalent Safety, Health and Welfare at Work acts, we find very broad and general demands protecting 'so far as is reasonably practicable' the safety and health at work of all employees. Employers are asked to provide information, instruction, training and supervision 'as is necessary to ensure so far as is reasonably practicable the safety and health at work of their employees.' This rather generous scope is not, however repeated in the specific regulations, which are listed below.

Employees are also asked to take responsibility for their health and safety, and manufacturers, designers and importers 'of any article or substance' must ensure that they are without risk to safety and health and that users are supplied with adequate safety and health information. Work places should be safe and without risk to health. The training requirement here is very important as it can decide whether or not management has been negligent in cases of accidents causing injuries to employees.

Employers must prepare a 'Safety Statement' which specifies the manner in which the safety and health of employees shall be secured at work. This has caused much confusion and it is hoped that a standard such as BS 7750 will take away the need for this rather vague demand. Readers should take care, however, to go on producing a safety statement for as long as it is requested, as it may take time for state health and safety inspectors to realize the implications and benefits to them of the standard.

A number of the 1993 directives are now listed, using the simple or shortened titles:

1. The Framework Directive.
   This updates the Safety, Health and Welfare at Work Act 1989 and a previous 1989 Framework Directive. It adds temporary workers to those who must be protected.
2. Workplace Directive.
3. Work Equipment Directive.
4. Personal Protective Equipment Directive.
5. Handling of Loads Directive.
6. VDU Directive.
7. Exposure to Carcinogens Directive.

Also underway at the time of writing were the following.

- Directive on Minimum Requirements for the Provision of Safety and/or Health Signs at Work.
  This updates an existing signs directive.
- Directive on the Minimum Safety and Health Requirements at Temporary or Mobile Sites.
  This would apply to all work places where even temporary construction or repairs are in progress.
- Directive on the Introduction to encourage Improvement in the Safety and Health at Work of Pregnant Workers and Workers who have recently Given Birth or are Breastfeeding.
  This could cause quite a bit of concern to personnel managers, especially where there is a large female staff.

The simple names for the above three are 'Safety and/or Health Signs', 'Construction Sites', and 'Pregnant and Breastfeeding Women'.

Directives are also in preparation concerning working hours (under dispute in the EC), young people at work, mines and quarries, offshore, vessels, transport of dangerous goods, exposure to dangerous substances, activities in the transport sector, fairgrounds and playgrounds.

If the workplace is a new building to be used for the first time after 31 December 1992, twenty requirements must be satisfied for health and safety. Many countries already have these as law under local building regulations. Looking down the list for possible new requirements after 1993, one sees the need to provide facilities for pregnant and breastfeeding women, changing rooms, and facilities for the disabled. When we look at the requirements for existing buildings, however, we find that all these must be added to the buildings within a certain timeframe. Actual new post-1993 requirements for new buildings relate to floors, windows, escalators, loading bays and overcrowding.

Once the structure is in place and satisfies the directive, the maintenance of equipment is called for, together with ventilation, temperature, lighting, traffic routes, sizes of toilets, and other relevant issues.

Work equipment must be safe and meet guidelines laid down in the work equipment directive. This also involves training. Users of VDUs are protected by a number of measures – keyboard, design, radiation, task and software design, timing, eye protection, and training. Workers lifting loads will do so properly and only in the weights allowed to suit their abilities. They will be trained in lifting. Personal protective equipment will be available and be in use wherever required and there will be full training in its use. Safety and health signs will be displayed where and as they are required, and there will be first aid facilities, and both facilities and procedures for pregnant and breastfeeding women. All dangerous substances will be handled according to strict regulations.

Both the Framework directive and the new directives call for a 'Safety Statement'. This is giving employers some problems. In a number of cases insurance companies are not happy with a statement which they privately believe is not worth the paper it is written on. The problem is that most safety statements are indeed not worth the paper they are written on if they are not directly related to a system of management control.

The safety statement should be a copy of the Quality Policy Statement, relating to management's intention to operate a control system to ensure that all health and safety regulations, and all other health and safety targets set by policy, will be implemented, monitored and controlled. A safety statement will only be acceptable if it is cross-referenced to a management control system such as BS 7750 or ISO 9000.

In summary, all the health and safety regulations should be met fully, if one is to protect workers and to protect oneself legally. This will be achieved by implementing a control system under a standard such as BS 7750, and, above all, by training all staff. A management control system, verifiable by an independent standard, and a proven track record in staff training should ensure sound sleep for management as far as the health and safety regulations are concerned.

CHAPTER 19

Environmental Management Standards

The eco-management and auditing scheme regulation

From 1 January 1993 a voluntary EC Eco-scheme, under the above title, has been open to any company in the Community 'engaged in industrial activities at a given production site'. These words imply all manufacturing and certain distribution and service activities. Companies who do participate successfully will have the honour of being granted a logo for the specific site concerned. Names of participating companies will be published by the Commission – a kind of EC-wide honours list, called the Registered Members List.

This regulation is voluntary for participating companies for four years, which suggests that it may become compulsory after that date. It has, however, been compulsory from 1 January 1993 for each member state to set up a national infrastructure including an accreditation scheme. This is usually in the form of an environmental protection agency, although some countries may use their government's department of industry for the accreditation scheme. In describing the required agency, the Commission stated:

> Among other things, this agency is required to develop knowledge of the criteria, principles and appropriate methodologies to carry out audits, prepare suitable users' guides and launch awareness-raising and training activities targeted in particular on small firms.

Within twelve months from 1 January 1993, member states were expected to have the certification schemes up and running, so that the regulation 'applies with effect' from 1 July 1994.

Generally, the distinction between a directive or regulation and a standard is fairly straightforward. The standard allows a directive or regulation to be met, and a management system developed to a standard such as ISO 9000 or BS 7750 may allow whole sets of regulations and directives to be satisfied. So, how does one implement the demands of the Eco-scheme? These demands read like a prescription for the BSI standard BS 7750, the environmental management standard. Indeed BS 7750 itself carries tables cross-referencing it both to the Eco-scheme and to ISO 9000. Any company reading the requirements of the Eco-scheme would be hard pressed to find a system for its implementation without a structure such as that given by the BS standard.

To a large extent BSI is ahead of the field and having succeeded so spectacularly with BS 5750 – ISO 9000 – EN 29000, hopes to do it again with the green standard, BS 7750, with that standard becoming the basis for meeting the demands of the Eco-scheme regulation. Such hopes make good sense as BS 7750 appears to satisfy all of the demands of both the Eco-scheme and the health and safety regulations, and in turn all relevant EC and local environmental regulations.

ISO has been slow to develop a version of the green standard, using BS 7750 as the model, and one excuse has been that ISO was waiting for the EC Eco-scheme regulation to go through in 1993. However, an ISO standard is certainly expected.

The EC Eco-scheme is unusual, either as an EC directive or a regulation, as it is so detailed in its demands that it specifies almost as much as a full standard, not quite enough, however, when one looks closely. Many companies in Europe may simply take the Eco-scheme as both a voluntary directive and a standard and implement it.

The central demand of the Eco-scheme is for an 'environmental protection system'. This is the counterpart of the BS 7750 'Environment Management System'. This applies to a specified production site and involves a 'systematic, periodic evaluation of environmental performance'. Everything else demanded by the audit, from formal stated policy to a programme of site measures and a management system, is more than catered for in BS 7750. One area of different emphasis, described as a 'key element' is an environmental audit. Audits are called for in the BS standard but the Eco-scheme asks that this key element be followed up with an 'environmental statement'. This statement is expected to be supported by an independent audit and report, all of which must be made available to the public.

The Eco-scheme is designed 'to target motivated companies straight-away', to improve their environmental performances, and in its own words:

> The voluntary nature of the proposed approach is perfectly consistent with the objectives of the Commission which wishes at this stage to give an impetus to improvements in the performance of industrial operations, irrespective of size or nature, to encourage companies to behave responsibly and to facilitate the flow of information to, and participation by, the public, as an addition to the traditional regulatory approach.

This sounds very much like the beginning of a new ISO 9000 process, and will spread in the same way. One forms an impression that the authors of the Eco-scheme are using an element of proselytizing at this 'missionary stage', hoping that it will take hold and spread, at which time we can expect its voluntary nature to give way to either mandatory market pressures or regulations.

It further adds that the 'credibility of the voluntary scheme is guaranteed by systematic external verification carried out by an independent accredited auditor'. EN 29000, the European Norm for ISO 9000, is suggested as the standards structure. This is another hint that some of the authors expect that ISO 9000 will be expanded to embrace BS 7750 or its ISO or EN equivalents when they evolve.

The Eco-scheme is open to 'any company engaged in industrial activities at a given production site', and this applies also to service and distribution companies. The companies which participate, and the word 'participate' is used throughout the regulation, as if participation also embraces certification, will be granted a logo for the 'specific site' concerned. The participating companies will also be published in the official journal of the EC, the honours list, or EC-wide register of members.

All participating companies must satisfy these conditions:

- Carry out an environmental review of the site concerned.
- On the basis of the findings, introduce an environmental protection system, including the elements already mentioned and an audit procedure.
- After each audit, draw up an environmental statement intended for the public, the contents to include figures on performance, problems brought to light, policy objectives and future intentions.
- Have an accredited environmental auditor examine and validate the audit and the statement.

From 1 January 1993, each member state was obliged to put the following into effect:

Each Member State will ensure that steps are taken to introduce an accreditation system, responsible for establishing and applying appropriate procedures for the accreditation of the environmental auditors entrusted with the task of validating the audit process and the environmental report. The Member States may rely on existing bodies, but must observe the conditions and criteria specified by this proposal in the matter of competence and pluralism.

Now we will look at the world's first environmental management standard, which as it stands should satisfy the demands of the Eco-scheme regulation and more besides.

In April 1992 British Standards Institution published its second revolutionary international management standard, BS 7750, the Environment Management Standard. Its first was the famous BS 5750, the model for ISO 9000. If you have ISO 9000, it means that you are operating a quality management system which ensures the conformance of your product to a specified level of quality. You can, however, manufacture a quality product to the ISO 9000 standard and damage both the environment and your staff. If you adopt also the BS 7750 standard, you will have achieved the ultimate standard – quality products and services produced and delivered in an environmentally caring manner.

The environment standard also covers the health and safety regulations, in that it incorporates control mechanisms which make it easy to administer both the environment and health and safety issues. This is a very important point, for while ISO 9000 and the environment standard are 'voluntary', the health and safety regulations are mandatory and are covered by legislation. The word 'voluntary' is in quotes because the other two standards are virtually mandatory when buyers demand them.

This means that ISO 9000 has already been surpassed, a fact that will shock most companies and elate a few. It has been surpassed by BSI, the very body which invented it in its model of BS 5750. The relationship between BS 7750 and environmental legislation illustrates the way standards interact with legislation.

BS 7750 is a mechanism for ensuring that the relevant environmental and health and safety regulations are complied with. On the environmental side these are all of the many pieces of environmental legislation being currently addressed by the EC Eco-scheme. On the health and safety side these are the 1989 directives updated by a number of specific 1993 regulations. BS 7750 is therefore a demonstrable system of environmental management control enabling the meeting of the regulations and allowing demonstration through certification. It will be embraced by companies looking for a target beyond ISO 9000 and by those already under pressure to produce evidence of environmental care. It will be a great prize for companies who want to use it to give them a market and PR advantage, starting in Europe. It will be particularly relevant for those selling into the EC public procurement market, for those selling to demanding buyers, and for those marketing products and services that are enhanced by environmental accreditation.

Once BS 7750 is universally adopted, false claims of environmental friendliness may be proscribed, so that the word 'environment' will not remain as demeaned as 'quality' was before the advent of ISO 9000.

Companies which have achieved ISO 9000 will find the new environment standard easier to implement than those which have not; at the same time it is possible to go for BS 7750 first, but whether one should do that depends on pressures from buyers. If buyers are demanding ISO 9000 first, then ISO 9000 is the only sensible route to the ultimate acheivement of both standards.

It is virtually certain that an ISO standard will follow to embrace BS 7750 and this was supposed to be underway after the adoption of the Eco-scheme, but progress appears to have been delayed. There is nothing, however, to stop any company in the world implementing BS 7750 as the first and only environment management standard. The first certification scheme was expected, at the time of writing, from the UK department of Industry in late 1993, but other member states were also setting up their own, as were private organizations.

ISO 9000 deals mainly with the control of the steps of production or services in the main product or service areas, while BS 7750 deals with the issues in the environment affected by product design, processing, end use and ultimate disposition, including packaging. BS 7750 also has immense legal significance as, partly by implication, partly directly, it calls for good ergonomic design for good ergonomic use and for product safety. It also incorporates health and safety for staff and emergency and accident prevention procedures – that is, public safety.

A quick sketch of the requirements of BS 7750 is that it calls for a register of environmental regulations, that is a record of what the rules are and for a system of management of the issues involved. For more details the reader may consult *BS 7750* the International Environment Management Standard, written by this author and published by Gower. That book also covers the EC Eco-scheme.

The main elements covered by both the EC regulation and the standard are as follows:

Emissions to the air.
Discharges to water resources.
Water supplies and sewage treatment.
Waste.
Nuisances.
Noise.
Radiation.
Amenity, trees and wildlife.
Urban renewal.
Physical planning.
Environmental impact assessment.
Product use.
Packaging.
Materials use.
Energy use.
Public safety.
Staff health and safety.

Air emissions

There are two main areas of activity affected by regulations on emissions to the air. The first relates to plant or factory operations, while the second relates to transport fleets. Most of these regulations are legal requirements, which means that they are supported by statutory instruments.

Typical legislation applying to the air emissions of plants includes regulations concerning the length of time during which smoke of varying densities may be emitted, and emissions of sulphur dioxide, suspended particulates, lead and nitrogen dioxide. Regulations also apply to the use of smokeless heating systems in built up areas, and to the sulphur content of gas oil. The EC council regulation No. 3322/88 relates to certain chlorofluorocarbons and halons which deplete the ozone layer.

Water resources

The regulations in this area are likely to contain both a general prohibition against water pollution as well as provisions for the licensing of direct and indirect discharges, in addition to water quality standards and those of managing water resources.

Water here may mean both inland waters and ocean. Specific regulations make it an offence to deposit deleterious matter, usually defined, in waters. Harbour waters and territorial waters are protected from dumping or discharges, while a number of regulations refer to the operation of ships and tankers, to oil discharges and to dumping at sea.

Certain substances also attract regulations. Examples of these are cadmium, mercury and hexachlorocyclohexane.

Water supplies and sewage treatment

The regulations in this area apply both to water supply companies and to private enterprises. They prohibit the contamination of any stream or reservoir used as a public water supply or any aqueduct or any other part of the supply system. It is an offence to allow pipes and other related devices to be out of repair and to cause or allow contaminated water or impurities to enter the water supply system.

Companies may feel that they have little responsibility here, but even the state of their own cisterns used for the supply of internal drinking water will be covered by a local authority regulation, which must be both in their register of regulations and under control to satisfy the standard.

Various water quality regulations, such as the European Communities (Quality of Water intended for Human Consumption) Regulations, also remind us that food and drinks manufacturers must be fully aware of both the regulations covering the state of their water and the controls exercised to ensure that the required quality of the water is maintained.

A large number of chemical substances are prohibited for discharge into waste or ground water systems. This area is known as effluent or other discharges, while licences are needed for controlled amounts of less damaging substances.

Waste

A number of regulations, including several made under the European Communities Act, apply to waste. These apply as follows.

Making local authorities responsible for the planning, organization, authorization and supervision of waste operations in their areas and for the preparation of waste management plans. They may also issue permits to treat, store and tip waste.

The 1982 EC toxic waste regulations make local authorities responsible for the planning, organization and supervision of operations for the disposal of toxic and dangerous waste in their areas and for the authorization of the storage, treatment and depositing of such waste. Local authorities are required to prepare special waste management plans. The regulations provide for permits to store, treat or deposit toxic and dangerous waste.

Local authorities are also responsible for the planning, organization and supervision of operations for the disposal of waste oils and the authorization of disposal arrangements. They can also provide permits for the disposal of waste oil.

Although companies may be involved with their local authorities in all of the above, the following regulations may apply directly to individual companies in the EC, with similar legislation elsewhere.

The first are the European Communities (Waste) Regulations 1984. These provide for the safe disposal and transformation operations necessary for regenerating polychlorinated biphenyls, polychlorinated terphenyls and mixtures containing one or both substances.

The European Communities (Transfrontier Shipment of Hazardous Waste) Regulations 1988 provide for an efficient and coherent system of supervision and control of the transfrontier shipment of hazardous waste. These regulations apply both to exports and imports. They prohibit holders of waste from commencing a transfrontier shipment until a notification has been sent to the appropriate authorities and duly acknowledged. A consignee in the state is prohibited from accepting hazardous waste from outside the state for disposal in the state unless it is accompanied by the appropriate acknowledgment. Carriers are prohibited from handling such wastes unless the waste is accompanied by the appropriate documentation.

Chemicals and pharmaceutical companies amongst others are affected by various national and international Dumping at Sea Acts. These in turn refer back to the Convention for the Prevention of Marine pollution by Dumping from Ships and Aircraft, 1972 (the Oslo Convention) and the Convention for the Prevention of Marine Pollution by Dumping of Wastes and other matters, 1972 (the London Dumping Convention). The acts prohibit the dumping of substances and materials from all vessels, aircraft and marine structures (for example, offshore platforms) anywhere at sea unless such dumping is carried out under and in accordance with a permit issued by the appropriate local authority.

Dumping at sea outside of territorial waters is permitted only if such dumping takes place under and in accordance with a permit granted by another state that is a party to the London or Oslo Conventions.

Other national regulations in the waste area cover local litter regulations, certain kinds of advertising, and the disposal of abandoned vehicles.

Nuisances

There are a number of interesting national regulations under this heading of relevance to companies in both manufacturing and service. They deal with a wide variety of nuisances affecting public health and the general environment. Typical nuisances could be offending pools, ditches, watercourses, drains, accumulations and deposits. Temporary dwellings, such as caravans, lean-tos and vehicles may be included also.

Noise

These regulations are also of great relevance to both manufacturing and service companies. First some EC examples.

European Communities (Construction Plant and Equipment) (Permissable Noise Levels) Regulations, 1988

These regulations give legal effect to EC directives on the approximation of the laws of the EC member states relating to the permissable noise levels of construction plant and equipment, for example, compressors, tower cranes, welding generators, power generators, powered hand-held concrete breakers and picks, hydraulic excavators, rope-operated excavators, dozers, loaders and excavator-loaders, designed for use in or about civil engineering or building sites.

European Communities (Lawnmowers) (Permissable Noise levels) Regulations, 1989

These regulations give legal effect to EC directives on the approximation of the laws of the member states relating to permissable noise levels of motorized mowers.

Radiation

There are a number of EC and national regulations covering the important matter of control of radiation.

Council Regulation (Euratom) No. 3954/87 of
22 December 1987

This regulation lays down maximum permitted levels of radioactive
contamination of foodstuffs and of feeding stuffs following a nuclear
accident or any other case of radiological emergency.

Council Regulation (EEC) No. 3955/87 of 22 December 1987

This regulation sets out the conditions governing imports of agricultural products originating in third countries following the accident at
the Chernobyl nuclear power station. This expired in 1989 but is an
example of a regulation which could be repeated in the case of a nuclear
accident.

European Communities (Medical Ionizing Radiation)
Regulations, 1988

These regulations provide that all those engaged in the use of ionizing
radiation for medical and dental purposes must be competent in
radiation protection measures and have appropriate training. The
exposure of a patient to ionizing radiation must be medically justified
and the dose to the patient must be as low as is reasonably achievable.

Amenities, trees and wildlife

There will be a large number of national regulations covering trees,
parks, amenities, landscape and wildlife. Samples from these showing
how companies may be affected are now given.

Companies may find that they are obliged to trim and cut hedges and
trees in some instances and are prohibited from doing so in others.
Certain categories of trees are exempt from any cutting. In making plans
for development, companies have to be aware of regulations concerning
the preservation of specified trees and other amenities, including
spaces, and of requirements to plant trees, shrubs and other plants and
for the landscaping of structures or land.

There are numerous wildlife regulations, the objectives of which are the protection and conservation of wild fauna and flora and for the conservation of areas having specific wildlife values. Apart from the regulations which demand protection of local wildlife, others may face companies which are involved in any way with materials or components made from the fur, skins or parts of wild animals, birds or certain species of flora. Even common lizards and newts are involved.

Urban renewal/site dereliction

A company may find itself in two different kinds of situation here. First, where it controls buildings or lands designated for urban renewal, or second where it has derelict sites or buildings in dilapidated or ruinous condition which might injure the health or safety of the neighbourhood.

A company may also own or occupy designated buildings listed for preservation for historical, cultural or architectural reasons.

Physical planning

All companies engaged in acquiring, constructing and expanding buildings must operate under physical planning regulations managed by local authorities. These lay down the requirements for permission, plans, sizes, heights and so on. Within these are the important Environmental Impact Assessment (EIA) directives. These are fundamental to the environment as they relate to the planning permissions of any development above a certain cost threshold.

The EC EIA Directive (85/337/EEC) applies to certain public and private projects and requires that those which are likely to have significant effects on the environment be subjected to assessment of such effects before development consent is given for them.

Environmental impact assessment

If one undergoes an environmental impact assessment study and fails to obtain planning permission, then the subject of operating to BS 7750 becomes irrelevant. If, on the other hand, one is facing an assessment for a new plant, this is an excellent time to begin planning for the standard as the work for the assessment may form the basis for both the proper future operation of the plant and its monitoring.

The local authority responsible for issuing planning permission for the project usually commissions an independent third party to carry out an environmental impact audit on the likely effects of the proposed project. The auditing body may use both baseline studies and predictive techniques to calculate the effects of the proposed project on such elements as air and water, quality, health, nuisance and noise.

Council Directive (85/337 EEC) sets out the projects subject to assessment. They include virtually all plants in process industries, those in extractive industries such as mining, energy producing installations and metal processing. Also included are chemical, food, textiles, wood, paper, leather, rubber and certain infrastructural projects.

The likely outputs agreed between the project proposer and the assessment agency can, if they fall within the limits set by regulations, become the targets for achievement within the subsequent operating environment. These can be set as limits beyond which the company does not intend to stray, while the limits set by the regulations can be the extreme upper limits. Staying within these and preferably at the level set in the assessment, or even lower, can be the levels set for compliance with the standard.

Product use

This is a most interesting issue, and the reader needs to be informed that this interpretation comes from an early reading of the standard shortly after its publication at a time when companies were first considering this aspect of the standard. Even if the standard authors did not specifically have product use in mind, it is probably the most important issue for many companies, as the safety, ergonomics and 'usability' of products are certainly now legal issues, covered increasingly by legislation. Elsewhere in this book, remarks about how health and safety regulations, and such issues as the usability of software in online processing situations, where there is a potential for accidents, should help make this point. Any reading of BS 7750, or indeed the latest version of ISO 9000, should offer convincing proof that these standards are a way of managing the end use of products and services, that is ensuring that they are used safely and properly, or at least educating users in these respects as far as possible. It should also offer the assurance that as a method of demonstration of a caring management system, one, at least, obtains the protection of a strong defence in cases of claims under product liability or charges of negligence.

Packaging

This important area is so affected by emerging EC legislation that a separate chapter (Chapter 20) is devoted to it.

Materials

The use of materials is an environmental issue. The review of materials needs to begin at the design of the product or service and its packaging, and ensure the careful use of materials, with the emphasis always on a reduction in the amount of materials used and the possibility of recycling. End users also need instructions in materials disposition, and such instructions can apply both to ordinary materials, such as glass and paper, and to the recycling of dangerous wastes, such as batteries.

Energy

One must design and implement an energy conservation programme, both for normal processing and for all the other activities, including office and transport, within the company. This area is so well developed that if one does not already have such a system, plenty are available 'off the shelf', or from the nearest national energy saving information agency. What the standard demands is that energy be treated as an issue and controlled accordingly.

Public safety

If there is a public safety issue, as there will be in many process plants, including chemicals and power stations, and in organizations distributing dangerous substances, a separate hazard and emergency control system, with all the accompanying emergency procedures, must be put in place. This is of such fundamental importance to both public safety and corporate and personal responsibility that unless the industry has codes of practice, control mechanisms and its own independent or government audits, an expert outside agency should be used. This issue makes an interesting point about the standard. The standard is a control and documentation mechanism, which at all times assumes expert management and control at the detailed level. It expects aircraft to be flown by pilots and to be maintained by engineers, who are in turn monitored by a management system.

Health and safety

These are very much a subset of the environment management system, but they are now compulsory in the EC and in many other parts of the world. Because of this, and because of the ease with which they can be fitted into, and accommodated by, the environment management system, they are, in fact, an excellent motivation for adopting BS 7750. They have been dealt with in detail in the previous chapter.

CHAPTER 20

Packaging
and the
Environment

One of the areas most affected by environmental legislation is that of packaging, and this applies to all manufacturers, distributors, retailers and, most of all, packaging manufacturers. The most important issue facing the packaging, distribution, and retailing industries is the proposed EC directive on packaging and packaging waste. This will affect both producers of packaging and its users.

The objective of the legislation is to reduce the overall impact of packaging waste on the environment by the following means: to reduce the amount of materials used, to encourage recovery and recycling, and to minimize the amounts of waste going to landfill. The targets are as follows:

Within 10 years of the directive becoming law, 90 per cent by weight of packaging waste output must be removed from the waste stream to be recovered.

Germany did not wait for this EC directive, and by 1 January 1993 all packaging, including consumer, had to be produced from environmentally tolerable materials and the minimum amounts of packaging had to be used. To the dismay of many non-German suppliers, manufacturers and retailers are obliged to take back transport packaging, which must be reused and not dumped. The system is identified by green dots and is known as the German Green Dot Code. The comparable EC directives are known as 'Eco-labelling' as they will set up a marking or labelling system for the recovery of packages.

Packaging companies in particular are quite alarmed by the speed of the legislation and the bad press given to the package. Their products are now under scrutiny worldwide. Many are less worried about the Eco-labelling directive, than they are about the directive on packaging waste, and particularly the hard line taken by Germany, which is seen almost as an infringement of the rules of the internal market by setting standards and deadlines that appear to go beyond emerging norms. In some member states over 80 per cent of packaging waste goes to landfill. By the year 2000 all member states will have to reduce this to 10 per cent, but Germany wants even this demanding schedule speeded up.

Senior managers within the packaging industry believe that the environment is probably the single greatest challenge of the 1990s facing them. They are not slow to say that the German 'Topfer Decree', which requires that industry as opposed to local authorities must collect and recycle between 40 per cent and 60 per cent of all packaging waste by the end of 1993, with this figure moving up to 80 per cent by the end of 1995, imposes almost impossible targets and unreasonable implementation dates. What this decree means in practice is that after the goods come out of the package, the packaging company is responsible for the collection and disposition of the package, and this has already had the effect in Germany of so much being collected that the mills cannot cope with it and huge quantities are exported to neighbouring countries – a warning perhaps about the unforeseen effects of regulation.

The EC Packaging Waste Directive should moderate the German system, but it will still have a very significant effect, making member states find new ways to recover 90 per cent of waste for incineration, recycling, composting or by newly-invented methods.

Printing is also affected, as another proposed piece of legislation, which will impact on both the print and packaging industries, is the directive on the control of solvent emissions. This directive provides for measures and procedures to limit the emission of organic solvents from certain industries, including the printing industry.

Many senior packaging industrialists believe that the full truth about packaging is not being told, and, in particular, that we are ignoring the other side of the packaging debate – not the package as a thing to be environmentally recycled, but a device for protecting and carrying the product. Dr Hans Rausing, the chairman of the Tetra Laval Group, spoke at a 1992 London *Financial Times* conference on the subject.

In his words the facts are that the food industry and food distribution could not take place without packaging. Secure food supply to all the places in the world that are fortunate to have a food supply needs packaging. One reason why food cannot get to many parts of the world, is a shortage of packaging. A correct package saves more than it costs. And apart from the absolute necessity of having a package for such a vital substance as milk, if it is to be transported at all, contamination, poisoning and disease are reduced and eliminated by packaging.

Other spokespersons believe that between 30 per cent and 50 per cent of food can be spoiled in the third world before reaching its destination, because of bad packaging. Through careful design packaging can be both useful and reusable and packaging organizations recommend the following guidelines:

- Avoid all claims of environmental care not supported by certification.
- Assess all the environmental factors in choosing a pack, particularly: energy and raw material requirements throughout the distribution chain, waste arising at all stages through the distribution chain; expected impact on post-consumer waste.
- Can we use secondary materials? For example, a higher level of recycled fibre for corrugated cases, low-quality recycled paper for internal memos, recycled plastics for non-food contact containers.
- Do not use excessive packaging.
- Design litter reduction into products and services. Include litter warnings on packages.
- Encourage repeat use where appropriate, such as pallets and carrier bags.
- Design or subcontract recycling processes.

CHAPTER 21

General Legal Liability

ISO 9000 is a voluntary standard, in that there is no direct legal requirement to adopt it. It is similar to its sister standard, from the BSI stable, BS 7750, the environmental management standard, in this respect. But as we have seen, both standards may as well be compulsory if buyers demand them. Now however, it is important to demonstrate that even voluntary standards can become a legal requirement in one or more ways. First when they are the only practical way of satisfying the demands for conformance to a compulsory regulation, or of demonstrating such conformance. Second, where by becoming a code of practice, that is the best way of doing things, they become the method of demonstrating the kind of careful management that protects one from product liability or charges of negligence.

When a standard attracts a regulation, which, for example in Europe these days, is usually based on an EC directive, it becomes compulsory. We recognize it in individual countries by its statutory instrument, or its act of parliament, name and number. There are, however, as we have shown, very few compulsory standards over and above the national metrology or measurement standards, which if abused expose one to charges of fraud.

Now new EC directives, backed by legislation in the member states, are adding a new impetus to the standardization process, by setting up regulations which are difficult to implement and control without an overall management control system, or, put another way, difficult to demonstrate conformance to without a demonstrable system of internal verification. And an outstanding example of this can be seen in the new health and safety regulations, which are difficult to implement and manage without an overall control system such as ISO 9000 or BS 7750.

The health and safety regulations are directed at users, where they apply to end products. Where those products end up at the user sites subject to health and safety regulations, they become key environmental issues for the manufacturers of those products, every bit as important to the environment as emissions, effluent discharges and toxic waste. Two such regulations of interest to computer hardware and software producers are, as we have seen, the VDT directive and the emerging software ergonomics directive. These are excellent examples of how both regulations and codes of practice relate to each other and to standards. We will look at these shortly.

Where ISO 9000 (BS 5750) is customer or market-driven, BS 7750 is driven also by strong legal and insurance motivations. This is because it is an ideal vehicle for both the health and safety regulations and the very important issues of product liability and public safety. The management system called for in the standard caters for all of these. While ISO 9000, in its latest draft, makes idealistic statements, or aspirations, about these issues, it does not yet provide a mechanism for their control. That will come when ISO publishes the new standard which will integrate BS 5750 and 7750. This writer, therefore, has interpreted this state of affairs as one in which the only legal protection available, both corporately and individually, against claims under product liability and possible unjustified charges of negligence is through the adoption of BS 7750.

If one infringes measurement standards, by cheating on vodka dispensers or gas pumps, one faces the risk of committing fraud. In the area of products and services, however, only the few compulsory standards, such as those covered by the EC directives, exist. The emergence of both the health and safety regulations and the environment standard has now changed the legal situation significantly.

A product may state that it conforms to a standard, and if that claim is incorrect the standards authority can disown it. To smooth the process of accreditation, many international and national standards authorities have certification schemes, through which they issue certificates of accreditation to products which meet the standard. In industry it is virtually impossible to sell a component unless it is certified to a standard; in the medical and pharmaceutical industries it is impossible to sell a product in the western world unless it is registered as certified with appropriate health authorities. Other sectors which demand certification are electronics, electrical, telecoms, and construction.

Many of the new EC directives, backed by legislation in the member states, are setting up regulations which are difficult to implement and control without an overall management control system, or put another way, difficult to demonstrate conformance to without a demonstrable system of internal verification. An outstanding example of this can be seen in the new health and safety regulations.

Product use or usability is becoming a major new area of interest to manufacturers. This will be illustrated shortly with software.

The health and safety regulations are directed at users, where they apply to end products – products such as medical, electrical, software. Where such a product ends up at the user sites subject to health and safety regulations, for example, a potentially dangerous piece of machinery, it becomes a key environmental issue for the manufacturer of that product, every bit as important to the environment as emissions, effluent discharges and toxic waste. A number of products can be used to illustrate the points being made here, and these include all electrical devices, building components and machinery, but the most outstanding product for this purpose is software.

Two regulations affecting software, one law at the time of writing and the other emerging, are the EC VDT regulation and the emerging software ergonomics directive. It is necessary to drive home a point here to avoid confusion. Software companies in common with meat factories, hotels and all other places of work have to implement such health and safety regulations as use of VDUs, good software, safe equipment, lifting of loads and safety signs; but because they are also the producers of products subject to one existing and one pending health and safety regulation they have the additional responsibility to ensure that their products are environmentally sound: as far as usage is concerned.

Usability and ergonomics as well as safety are environmental issues for them. Why is this so? Because their potential customers are being bound by law not to use these products if they do not conform to new regulations.

These regulations are going much farther than user-friendly VDUs and good layouts of menus. BS 7750 deals also with the prevention of accidents and responses to emergencies. The reading of data badly projected by inadequate software has been seen to be responsible for accidents in major process plants and with confusion in reading signals from aircraft engines. Imagine the potential for disaster in the running of a nuclear power station, should the software not be ergonomically sound. Product use is a key environmental issue for software developers, especially in situations where safety is critical.

ISO 9000 and BS 7750 are standards for management systems. Where in turn the product can be manufactured to a product standard, it is not conceivable that one can achieve these standards without at least also manufacturing the product to the appropriate product standard, or safety standard where a safety standard also applies. Basic examples are the standards for manufacturing concrete, and the IEC and EC regulations for the safe working of electrical equipment.

What this means is that if you are a hardware or software manufacturer your customers are now (from the beginning of 1993) bound by law to ensure that users of your products, over their VDUs, are catered for by your hardware or software in a manner which is within the VDT regulation, which is a legal health and safety issue for them, and a real environmental, marketing, and potential product liability and public safety issue for you. Also emerging is ISO 9241, the software ergonomics standard, which will lead to a new EC regulation, but which, simply because it is now in existence, will be an issue in product liability and will be automatically expected from software and hardware companies seeking either or both BS 7750 and the Eco-scheme logo.

If anyone doubts that there are public safety considerations with software or hardware, simply think of the number of critical online applications, including those with a potential for public danger, that both software and hardware support today.

To summarize, software companies and other suppliers of critical online equipment and systems, who may be clean and green and not burdened with such issues as emissions and discharges, have other critical environmental issues to deal with, chiefly product integrity, usability, and safety. In the language of quality management, the requirements are that software and hardware manufacturers should ensure that their products also satisfy individual product standards. ISO 9241 is to software companies what the IEC safety directives are to computer manufacturers. They must be met to ensure compliance with ISO 9000 or BS 7750.

Another interesting and instructive aspect of employer liability may be seen in the demands for both control and training in the health and safety regulations. It is very much in the interests of a company to implement these regulations, even where there has been a delay in local legislation, as the very existence of these EC directives can be used against employers in claims for damages or charges of neglect. The act of training employees also transfers some of the responsibility for their safety from management to their own shoulders. Above all however, is the point that demonstration of compliance to a control system such as BS 7750, which incorporates health and safety, public safety and good product use, is the very best defence, both corporately and individually, against claims under product liability and against mischievous charges of negligence. More and more both company lawyers and insurers are seeing this point.

In the case of software, for example, this means that a software developer trying to achieve ISO 9000 needs in the first instance to ensure that the products manufactured meet both the requirements of the EC VDT Regulation and ISO 9241, the software ergonomics standard. This applies to all new products supplied after 1 January 1993, with a time scale for adaptations of existing non-conforming products.

Finally, under the heading of legal liability we must deal with that important matter of liability for pollution or damage through accidents or 'occurrences', past or present, to the environment. This is a changing situation and many industries are anxious to avoid the kind of repressive legislation seen in the US Superfund law.

The approach taken here is to ignore the complexities of the laws and their potential consequences and to deal instead entirely with insuring against such risks. How this may be done in six of the twelve member states now follows. Readers in the other six states will need to consult their local insurance companies, as only the information given now was available at the time of writing. (All of the following material was kindly supplied by André D. Hellebuyck, Vice President of AIG Europe in Brussels, and Chairman of the ICC Working Party on Insurance/ Environment Issues.)

Environment impairment liability (E12) insurance coverage in Europe

France

There is an insurance 'pool' under the name of 'ASSURPOL', constituted by 49 insurers and 14 reinsurers, offering a capacity of FF125,000,000 on a 'claims made' insurance basis. The pool can offer a capacity of up to FF165,000,000 and, in exceptional cases, the Italian pool Inquinamento can offer additional capacity for French insurers. For 1992, the annual premium income of ASSURPOL amounted to approximately FF20,000,000 for about 320 policies.

Italy

Since the end of 1979, the Italian insurers have had a pool, by the name of INQUINAMENTO. Their capacity amounts to LIt.50,000,000,000, of which 20,000,000,000 is directly assumed by a group of 78 insurance companies and 30,000,000,000 is provided by a number of reinsurers, among which the German reinsurer Frankona takes a leading role.

Outside Germany, the pool INQUINAMENTO is the best performing European facility for environmental impairment insurance.

The Netherlands

Gradual pollution is coverable only under the MAS pool's policies. MAS (Milieu Aansprakelijkheidsverzekering Samenwerkingsverband) was established in 1984 and is a reinsurance mechanism, constituted by 60 companies. They offer capacity of NLG17,000,000. It functions on the basis of 'claims made' coverage.

Denmark

Since March 1992, about 15 insurance companies put together the Danish pool. It offers a capacity of DKK70,000,000 and issues coverage on a 'claims made' basis, which is the standard for all general liability insurance in Denmark.

As opposed to the policies issued in the United States, the Danish and Italian policies exclude from the coverage pollution that occurred prior to the inception of the policy. An AIG policy covers the 'unknown past'.

United Kingdom

As of 1990, most UK general liability policies exclude coverage for pollution, except if such pollution is 'sudden and accidental'. A rather explicit clause is written in to most policies to that effect. Also, the London reinsurance market decided to discontinue any coverage for gradual pollution. This has an impact on foreign insurance companies that wish to reinsure themselves on the London market and on foreign reinsurers who often place 'retrocessions' on the London market (reinsurance for reinsurers).

The UK is now witnessing a growing number of cases where firms, facing considerable clean up expenses, try to call upon past insurance policies issued over a long period of time.

Germany

This is the most interesting European country from a pollution insurance point of view. The German general liability policies all have a standard basic wording, which can be extended by means of endorsements broadening its scope. The standard wording operates on an 'occurrence' basis and the only exceptions to that rule are some policies covering product liability for exports to the USA, in which, only in exceptional cases, part of the coverage works on 'claims made' basis.

The standard German general liability wording gives coverage for sudden and accidental property damage caused by pollution, but specifies that as regards bodily injury, coverage is also effective for the consequences of gradual pollution. This has applied for several decades.

In 1960, a new law 'Wasserhaushaltsgesetz', or WHG (Water Resources Protection Act), introduced into Germany a strict liability for damage to water resources caused by underground storage tanks. Any water pollution that occurred or gradually built up during the last few decades is likely to become evident and will eventually result in a claim under WHG liability insurance policies.

In 1991 the Federal Environmental Agency introduced a new law, expanding the strict liability for damage to water resources to damage also to soil and air. This new law goes along with a determination of a maximum amount of legal liability for each individual classified installation of DM160,000,000 for both property damage and bodily injury. The new law also has a provision for compulsory insurance for the 96 types of classified installations listed in an annex thereto. The compulsory insurance requirement does not apply yet and a specific ordinance to that effect has to be made.

In view of this new legislation, the German accident insurers managed to introduce a new policy that, as of 1 January 1993, gradually replaces the former policies and for which the trigger is the 'manifestation' of the damages. Possibly, the German insurers can continue to afford up to DM160,000,000 worth of coverage on that basis for their largest clients. But the question remains whether this is reasonably affordable for smaller operators.

The German insurers also agreed to cover the risk caused by so called 'normal operations' (Normalbetrieb), which refers to a new law which imposes strict liability on the operator of an installation that meets the safety and environmental requirements set forth by the authorities and does not cause emissions above the legally permitted levels. This is in case it transpires that operations that today seem perfectly legitimate cause harm to the environment in the future and the operator will be held liable for the damage. Such risk is a pure 'development risk'. German insurers have agreed to include coverage for this development risk in their new policy, provided the insured can prove, when damage becomes manifest, that, at the time when he conducted the operations that caused the damage, the state of development of scientific knowledge would not have permitted him to know or foresee that his operations would cause harm.

In so doing, it would seem the German insurers have reached the limit of what is insurable. For that extension to their coverage, it is felt today that the maximum limit of liability that can be insured for any one installation could not exceed DM30,000,000. This would today be the maximum capacity of the German insurance market for that aspect of their new Pollution Liability Insurance. The intention is to start introducing this new policy for new operations, operations that considerably change the nature of their business, operations that change insurers, or operations that have had claims paid.

The conversion entails the exclusion of all pollution liability from general liability policies and the integration of all pollution liability coverage in a specific environmental impairment liability policy. In so doing, the German market will reach a situation comparable to the situation prevailing in the USA and Italy, where the only way to get pollution coverage is to buy such a specific policy. The only major difference between Germany and the USA and Italy will be the number of coverages involved.

PART IV

The Infrastructure

Trans-European Networks and Information Databases

The information supplied here was kindly given by the European Commission. Fuller details can be obtained in the published booklets *Introducing Eurobases* and *Directory of Public Databases*.

There will be a number of ways to access these in the member states, including direct subscription to each service. Information and access will be available both in local EC offices and in agencies reporting to ministries of industry and trade. Outside of the EC, any good technical information agency or library will know what to do.

CELEX (Comunitatis Europeae Lex)

CELEX is the interinstitutional computerized documentation system for Community law. It covers community legislation including treaties, acts, and secondary legislation, case law of the Court of Justice, documents of the Court of First Instance; preparatory acts; parliamentary questions; and national provisions implementing directives.

ECLAS (European Commission library automated system)

Database of the central library of the European Commission, namely a bibliographical database of the works and documents available in Commission departments, covering all aspects of European integration. The following are included: monographs, periodical articles, Community publications, non-legislative documents from the Commission's 'COM series', publications by international organizations such as the UN, OECD, NATO, EFTA, ILO, IMF, WHO, GATT, and so on.

Eurocron (Statistics)

Statistical data stored in tables and covering the most important sectors of the social and economic climate in the member states of the Community. This statistical information is subdivided into the following three data-sets.

- Eurostatistics comments on and publishes the main economic and social indicators needed to analyse short-term trends in the economic activity of the 12 member states, the Community as a whole, and the USA and Japan.
- Regiostat contains a harmonized selection of regional statistics up to Level 2 of the nomenclature of territorial statistical units (NUTS). The indicators selected are designed to provide a basic macroeconomic analysis at regional level.
- Farmstat provides a summary of the main results of the 1987 survey of the structure of agricultural holdings in the member states. The purpose of the data is to facilitate structural analysis and comparison of agriculture in the member states.

Info 92 (Information on the single market)

This is a factual and bibliographical database on progress towards the single market as it relates to the Commission's White Paper, together with summaries of Community legislation adopted and in the course of preparation.

The database is broken down into three areas:

- Removal of physical barriers.
- Removal of technical barriers.
- Removal of fiscal barriers.

Info 92 also covers the progress of the incorporation of Community legislation into the member states' own national law, together with a news update on figures and current events relating to the implementation of the White Paper.

Rapid (Spokesman's Service of the European Commission)

Rapid gives rapid access to press releases and information issued by the Spokesman's Service of the European Commission. It contains the full text of all documents issued by the Spokesman's Service: press releases, information memos, event memos, speeches, key documents.

SCAD (Community system for accessing documentation)

SCAD is a bibliographic database that includes the lists of the following documents: Commission proposals and acts, parliamentary reports, resolutions, council resolutions, community legislation, published articles dealing with the activities of the Community.

Sesame (R&D, demonstration and technology projects)

A documentary database containing descriptions of energy research and development projects, demonstration and hydrocarbons technology projects under Community programmes managed by the Directorate-General for Science, Research and Development (DG XII), the Directorate-General for Energy (DG XVII) and member states.

ABEL (Amtsblatt elektronisch)

ABEL is a bibliographical database which can be used to search, select and order documents from the *Official Journal of the European*

Communities. ABEL contains the tables of contents archived in the Arcdon system (optical archives). The documents are entered in the base on the day of publication of the *Official Journal.*

ABEL is a document delivery service of the Office for Official Publications of the European Communities.

AGREP (Permanent inventory of agricultural research projects in the European Communities)

AGREP is a factual database containing the titles of publicly financed research projects in agriculture, forestry, fisheries and foodstuffs going on in the member states of the EC. Only ongoing projects are listed, and the normal lifetime of projects is about five years.

BACH (Base for the accounts of companies harmonized)

BACH contains statistical data on aggregate company accounts. Using information supplied by the balance sheet analysis centres in the various countries and then harmonized, this database provides chronological information on the aggregate accounts of 22 sectors and three size categories of companies in 10 countries.

BIOREP (Biotechnology research projects in the European Community)

BIOREP is a factual database containing a permanent inventory of biotechnology research projects undertaken in the member states of the European Community.

CATEL (Electronic catalogue of the Office for Official Publications of the European Communities)

CATEL is a bibliographical database from which publications and documents of the Community institutions, and documents published in the *Official Journal of the European Communities,* L Series, and Court of Justice notices in the L Series can be sought, selected and ordered.

CCL-Train (Common command language training)

CCL-Train is the training database that enables users to become familiar with online information retrieval and more particularly with use of the common command language (CCL).

CCL-Train contains summaries of scientific and technical publications dealing with subjects such as nuclear technology, safety engineering, agriculture, information, economics, law, medicine science, and so on.

COMEXT

COMEXT is the database for statistics on the European Community's external trade and trade between the member states.

CORDIS (Community research and development service)

This contains information on the Community's research and development programmes. There are a number of CORDIS databases covering such specifics as programmes, projects, news, partners, publications, and results.

Cronos (Macroeconomic statistics)

Cronos is a statistical database containing macroeconomic data covering all aspects of the economic and social situation in the EC member states. Statistics are also available for the USA, Japan, and around 150 countries.

DOMIS (Directory of materials data information sources)

DOMIS is a directory of sources and services available in Europe relating to information on materials. It is mainly intended for users working in industry, research or administration and provides details of the specialist information sources existing in the materials field.

ECDIN (Environmental chemicals data and information network)

Factual database on chemicals products liable to react with the environment. ECDIN collects information on all chemicals compounds manufactured and marketed on a large scale in the European Community, the USA and Japan. The information concentrates on the harmful effects of the substances and also lists all the properties which might help the user to assess the real or potential risks of a product and its economic and ecological impact.

ECHO NEWS (Online version of *ECHO news*)

ECHO NEWS, a full-text database, is the online version of the fortnightly publication of the same name put out by ECHO (European Commission Host Organization), a service provided by the Commission Directorate-General for Telecommunications, Information Industries and Innovation (DGXIII).

ECU (European currency unit)

Latest daily ECU rates in main currencies.

EPOQUE (European Parliament online query system)

European Parliament documentary database containing: references for all the documents compiled or examined by the European Parliament and for studies produced by the European Parliament and the national parliaments; the European Parliament Library catalogue; legislative procedures: references and stages reached.

ESPRIT (European strategic programme for R&D in information technology)

An online database of current ESPRIT projects.

Eurocontract (Partners for research projects)

Eurocontract is a factual database set up by the European Commission to help European organizations find partners with whom they can participate in the various research programmes. The information in the databases is closely linked to the specific calls for proposals which are issued regularly by the Commission, with details of the organization concerned, the name and address of a contact person and information either on a specific project for which partners are sought or on the organization's field of interest.

I'M GUIDE (Electronic information in Europe)

I'M GUIDE provides detailed information and is available in Europe via:

1. Electronic information products, such as databases, databanks, CD-ROMs, and so on, giving number of documents, language, abstract, producer, vendor, and so on.
2. Organizations such as DB and CD-ROM producers, host organizations, brokers, publishers with their name, address, network access and activities.

INFOMARK (Information market)

The information market database is the online version of the information periodical published at the initiative of Commission DG XII (Telecommunications, Information Industries and Innovation). Information market provides information on the latest innovations in the information and high technology markets.

Regio (Regional statistics)

Regio is Eurostat's database for regional statistics and covers the main aspects of economic and social life in the Community: demography, economic accounts, employment, unemployment, and related.

TED (Tenders electronic daily)

Tenders electronic daily is an online directory of invitations to tender for public works and supply contracts, not only from the 12 EC member states but also from the African, Caribbean and Pacific (ACP) countries associated with the EC, non-associated countries carrying out projects financed by the European Development Fund (EDF) and, under GATT, from Sweden, Japan, and USA, and elsewhere. TED is the online version of the S Series supplement to the *Official Journal of the European Communities*.

It contains all invitations to tender for public contracts published under Council Directives 2/62 and 305/71, that is:

1. Public supply contracts worth more than ECU 200,000.
2. Public works contracts worth more than ECU 5,000,000.
3. GATT invitations to tender worth more than ECU 130,000.
4. Service contracts worth more than ECU 200,000.

XIII MAGAZINE (Online version of *XIII Magazine*)

XIII Magazine is written by journalists, independent experts and representatives of EC institutions and other organizations active in communications and information technologies. The aim of this magazine is to provide information covering the activities and programmes supported by DG XIII.

ECHO

Finally, to help in accessing any or all of the above, and other EC databases, the Commission has a service called ECHO. This is a non-commercial organization offering access to unique databases and databanks, either wholly or partly sponsored by the EC, which are not available on any other online host service.

CHAPTER 23

The
Electronic
Marketplace

There are few areas of high technology where Europe is ahead of the United States. One of these is in the use of videotext, where a recent count of eight million videotext users in the world put 1.5 million in the US and 6.5 million in Europe. The reason, of course, is France with its 5.7 million Minitel terminals servicing 100 million hours of traffic each year. The France Telecom group, which owns Minitel, and the Teletex service over which it operates, have been responsible not just for the explosion of the electronic marketplace in France but for its spread to the rest of Europe and overseas.

So confident was Telecom France of the growth in Minitel use and services that Minitel sets were given out free in France, with customers paying only for the services to the service providers. Apart from videotext services such as Teletex, there are a host of other online information services, including some from a number of large providers such as McGraw Hill, Dunn and Bradstreet, Reuters and Bertelsmann, and thousands of smaller databases, all available worldwide over 650 real time information services. For information on some useful EC databases, see Chapter 22.

The market has been evolving away from specialized technical databases, such as medical and chemicals, to business information, market research and news, and, via services like Minitel, is now moving into entertainment, education, and the general interest market, embracing the home. A look at the thousands of service providers, offering their products over these systems reveals huge opportunities in this market, which has grown in Europe even in the face of recession. Supporting this process is the view of the European Commission that an open electronic marketplace is fundamental to the development of the internal market. Service suppliers outside Europe also see the 5.7 million Minitel user market in France (and approximately one million elsewhere in Europe) as a huge potential market for their services.

Minitel's promotional material reveals the versatility of the service and the huge range of its activities. One of its brochures describes the Minitel set or 'box' as follows: a strong box for banking, an information box for information, a phone box as a directory, a pay box for payroll, a signal box for ordering, a ticket box for reservations, a seed box for farming, and a gift box for selecting and buying gifts.

On the international front the gateway to the Minitel network, called 'Minitelact' is operated for France Telecom by Intelmatique. Intelmatique has now signed interconnection agreements with most foreign videotext networks. If a reader is a user of such a network, no extra subscription is needed to access the Minitel services. Interconnected networks are in the US, Japan, Switzerland, Portugal, Luxembourg, Italy, Finland, Spain, Denmark, Belgium, Germany, Holland and Ireland. These now have access to 16,000 service providers in their own countries. France also offers a '36 19' service, the French call number which offers access to foreign videotext networks, and enables service providers outside France to spread their services over the wider network. The server located outside France must either have an X25 access or access to a foreign videotext network. This gives the server the same advantages as a French supplier, and makes his services available on other non-French parts of the network. To get onto the '36 19' service, a potential service supplier needs to contact Intelmatique at 175, Rue du Chevaleret, 75013 Paris, France, Telephone + (33) 140 776840.

Another service called Quick Pass offers French service providers the possibility of making their services directly available on foreign videotext service networks interconnected with Teletex. It gives these services the same visibility as a local service. This service is also available in Belgium, Italy, Germany, Portugal, Finland, Switzerland and in the US, where it is operated by US West and Bell Atlantic. Service providers must sign a six month contract with Intelmatique.

Minitel is the leader in the exploding mass electronics marketplace. Together with other videotext services it is opening a new market for consultants who can help companies become service providers. In the space available here, all that can be done is to indicate the growth of this electronic marketplace. To explore it in detail would require an entire book.

A separate, but linked, market is that of electronic data interchange (EDI), also growing rapidly. In the chapter on selling to the multinationals it was noted that EDI may be required for doing business, in a paperless manner, with sophisticated buyers, but the growth of EDI itself is a phenomenon in Europe warranting attention. It is seen to be so important by the European Commission that a special programme called TEDIS, the Trade EDI Systems Programme, has been devoted to it.

The rationale behind TEDIS is that the Commission sees the free movement of information and data between member states as a vital prerequisite for the free movement of goods and services and for the development of cooperation between businesses on a European scale. The TEDIS programme prepares the way for the creation of pan-European networks which will allow the single market to function effectively. It wants to encourage a favourable environment for competitiveness by ensuring that developments in information and communication technologies are relevant to business. Administrative costs of doing business using paper are believed to be between 3.5 and 15 per cent of the value of goods.

The role of TEDIS is to coordinate EDI developments in different industry sectors and ensure their coherence in a multi-sectoral environment, and the rapid growth of EDI is seen to be symptomatic of the impressive wave of change and restructuring in the Community's industrial fabric. The Community wants to anticipate and cushion the impact of this ever increasing rate of technological and industrial change in order to turn it to best advantage, and it sees these changes not only affecting large manufacturers, but their component suppliers, many of whom are small businesses.

The TEDIS programme has an initial budget of ECU 5.3 million and had spent a further ECU 25 million between 1991 and 1994. The objectives have been:

- The integration of EDI implementations and activity in the member states across different sectors.
- The examination of the economic and social repercussions of EDI and its impact on the management of public and private companies.
- Increasing the awareness of potential users, particularly small businesses, and potential hardware, software or service providers.

This has involved continued work on the standardization of messages, the interconnection of value added data or network services, the establishment of secure EDI facilities and the creation òf an appropriate legal environment. Coordination has been assured at an international level through the United Nations and ISO.

Of high appeal to the Commission is the raising of the level of awareness of EDI. There will be regional awareness centres providing information and support at a local level and in the appropriate language to potential users in each member state, and the work of these centres will be linked and coordinated through the TEDIS programme.

EFTA is also fully involved, and attempts are underway to establish interfaces with the EDI systems of the Mediterranean and Central and Eastern European countries. The opening up of the modern market economies has placed a new emphasis on EDI to complement the new trading practices.

One may summarize the objectives of TEDIS in the Commission's own words from the latest TEDIS report:

As firms reorganise on a European scale to take full advantage of the Single Market of the future, Tedis has a dual role. Firstly it is essential that EDI standards and services exist at a European rather than at a purely national level. Secondly, it must make sure that the fragmentation into national markets is not replaced by a rigid electronic demarcation between different sectors of the economy. The EDI infrastructure must be both European and also integrate across all sectors. This infrastructure will be as important in the future European economy as the road and rail networks are today.

And on the difficulties and challenges that face the growth of EDI in Europe the Commission has stated:

There are still a number of difficulties facing the growth of trade electronic data interchange: EDI users must be guaranteed a high quality technical interconnection; the constraints and inadequacies of the member states' legal systems must be identified, and the storage methods, media and authentication methods analyzed from the legal point of view. The use of security techniques related to open EDI must be encouraged. Campaigns to raise awareness of the potential benefits of EDI must be coordinated and stepped up. Furthermore a specific inventory of EDI projects and applications in Europe must be drawn up. The creation of new Pan-European sectoral projects groups or initiatives from existing groups must be encouraged. Finally, there is an urgent need to assess the social and economic impact of the introduction of EDI in Europe.

All of which suggests fruitful work for researchers and consultants and PR people, who may get involved with TEDIS and related EDI programmes.

During 1992, TEDIS contracts were awarded to a wide variety of contractors, from computer consortia, to universities and private industry. ECU 500,000, for example, went to support a range of industry groups from fashion to construction, to promote and coordinate the development of EDI in their industry sector. Other contracts went to individual consulting companies. There were more calls for proposals during 1993 and the Commission says that there will be further invitations to tender in subsequent years.

So much for the establishment programmes, but EDI, and its sister service, electronic mail, or E.Mail, are also now a common feature of trading in the internal market. It is now seen as a key technique in managing the supply chain and it is also introducing other technologies, such as EPoS, electronic point of sale scanning, and EFTPoS, electronic funds transfer at point of sale. Many large retailers across Europe are now trading electronically with their suppliers. Typical in the UK are Tesco and Boots who use the INS-TRADANET EDI service. INS has a very large share of the total European market, perhaps as much as 35 per cent, making Britain a world leader in EDI.

This introduces the growing services of what are called the VANs, the value added networks, offering to handle all electronic contact between suppliers and customers. These will be both suppliers to large manufacturers and suppliers to major retail chains. The process tends to begin with the large customer, who, using a VAN, asks suppliers to come into the system and become paperless partners. The major VAN services in Europe are offered by SPRINT, GEIS, IBM, ICL, and INS.

It is forecast that the EDI market will grow to about ECU 400 million in 1995, or by 33 per cent per annum. By then network services will account for almost half of the total market, and Edifact will be the standard used for virtually all new applications, X 400 being the standard protocol.

The market leaders in Europe are GEIS and IBM, with AT&T Easylink and INS the leaders in the UK. The UK and the Netherlands are by far the most mature EDI markets. About two years behind them are France, Sweden and Germany.

CHAPTER 24

Testing and Certification

The harmonization of testing and certification services is a natural follow-on to the process of harmonizing standards. Where a single standard, or set, is agreed, this can have practical consequences only if common certification schemes exist, and if each national scheme is accepted throughout Europe or internationally.

The main purpose of harmonized certification is to allow products free access to the markets covered by the harmonization, so that repeat testing is not required in the countries of destination. The main mechanisms in Europe are legislation through EC directives, which become national law in each country, supported by harmonized product and management standards.

The main testing and certification processes in Europe, in the sense of the EC and EFTA, are to ensure the meeting of product standards, the meeting of the requirements of directives, which include compulsory standards, and the meeting of the requirements for quality management

and environmental management standards, and regulations such as the
EC Eco-scheme regulation.

As far as products in general, beyond those covered by directives, are
concerned, it is left to individual companies to meet their own testing
and certification demands. The market may also set the rules. Concrete,
for example, being daily poured into a major structure, will certainly be
expected to be tested daily by an independent concrete testing service,
which if the project is large enough may have a mobile test unit on site.
Most major buyers will demand formal evidence from their suppliers
that minimum product standards are being met. Apart from public
liability, there are other legal considerations, such as legislation
proscribing misleading advertising and product liability, which impose
obligations on companies to ensure the conformance of products,
including components, to their relevant standards.

Where directives do cover products, in certain categories covered by
compulsory directives, the only guarantee to the buyer that the products
conform is the CE Mark. This mark, placed upon a product, denotes that
it conforms to the requirements of all of the applicable EC directives and
that testing has taken place in accordance with rules laid down in the
directives. Up to now the most famous mark was the BSI kitemark,
known as such because of its shape. Now the Community has
introduced the CE Mark which should replace all others in those
categories needing this mark.

The CE Mark denotes that the product conforms to essential
requirements and is a 'passport' to European markets. It can be affixed to
any product that is 'fit for its intended use' according to the above. To
obtain the mark, the product must comply with the relevant ENs,
represented by a national standard, and have its fitness for use in
accordance with the above confirmed by an approved certification body.

The CE Mark is perhaps the supreme example of a product mark,
while ISO 9000 is that for a quality management system, and the Eco-
scheme that for environmental care. The CE Mark will eventually also
demonstrate conformance to an environmental standard, which will
mean that one will have to add the Eco-scheme to its list of
requirements.

An EN is of course the EC equivalent of what, up to now, were
national standards. A product qualifying for the CE Mark would have to
have all of its constituent components, which require individual
standards, already meeting those standards. An electrical device, for
example, could have a number of standards for its constituent parts,
while a pre-cast concrete beam will have such components as sand,

cement, lime, and aggregátes, all of which have separate product standards. Before meeting certain standards now, certification agencies are demanding that the plant have its quality management system also certified to ISO 9000.

Only certain categories of product need the CE Mark. Those covered by the directives in the following categories do:

- Electrical.
- Machinery (safety).
- Construction.
- Telecom.
- Medical.
- Personal protective equipment.
- Toys.

The CE mark denotes that the product conforms to essential requirements, such as those listed in the directives applying to the items above, and allows it into European markets. It is not, however, an indication of quality.

A good example of both the CE Mark and the directives it applies to is the Construction Products Directive which was implemented in 1991. It applied to all products to be used in a permanent manner in building or civil engineering works, and it laid down the following essential requirements.

- Mechanical resistance and stability.
- Fire safety.
- Hygiene, health, safety in use.
- Environmental.
- Protection against noise.
- Energy economy and heat retention.

The CE Mark can be affixed to any product that is 'fit for its intended use' according to the above. To obtain the mark, the product, as we have seen, must comply with the relevant ENs, represented by a national standard, and have its fitness for use in accordance with the above confirmed by an approved certification body. In the cases above, every single unit involved from cement to lime to aggregates must at the very least meet its individual national or equivalent EN standard, all required tests must be carried out, and all required certifications achieved. How the last is done is explained shortly.

The same rules for product standards as those above apply to companies wanting to be certified to ISO 9000, except that they will only be required to use the CE certification processes (to be explained shortly) for products covered by directives in the required categories. The ISO 9000 certification itself will, however, have to be achieved through a third party independent certification agency. There is at least one in each member state, usually also the national standards authority, although not necessarily so, and a number of private organizations who are now also accredited to certify to ISO 9000. While it is obvious that ISO 9000 will require conformance to whatever standards apply to the products in question, such as type, safety, and compatibility, simply because the customer will demand this, what has actually happened is that certification agencies are demanding ISO 9000 as a pre-condition to type approving products. This process has been accelerated by the emergence of the CE Mark.

Each national government establishes its testing and certification systems and notifies the EC Commission of the names of the agencies. These are known as 'Notified Bodies'. The 'Notified Bodies' can be certification agencies, test laboratories, and inspection agencies, usually appointed by government, although this is not yet clear. They are required to be totally independent and must conform to another set of European Standards known as the EN 45000 series, which have been put in place to provide a uniform system of accreditation across the EC.

The EOTC, European Organization for Testing and Certification, is the coordinating group attempting to ensure a uniform approach and rules.

The whole process is not without dangers and problems. The committees responsible for the harmonization and standards writing processes need to guard against 'groups of fanatics', as they are described by some, trying to impose unrealistic expectations. The standards advocates need a large constituency, which should include the market. They need to be practical and realistic and to provide a continuity in their participation.

Manufacturers inside and outside of Europe need to be aware that CEN, the European Committee for Standardization, is constantly at work devising new standards which become ENs. Once the EN is realized, all CEN states must comply with its requirements, and any outsider trying to sell into the relevant market without knowledge of the EN may become excluded, and will be excluded in the case of public procurement.

If, for example, local authorities are buying and the product sought is covered by a new EN, prospective suppliers must ensure that their offerings comply. This could require re-design, re-tooling and re-manufacture. If one is a European subsidiary or licensee of a US or Japanese company, this means both acquiring a knowledge of the evolving ENs and passing the information back to the principal.

This is the case for specific EN product standards, but for a management standard such as ISO 9000 or BS 7750, one may also find that codes of practice, however voluntary, are also expected to be adopted. A good example is ISO 9241, the software ergonomics standard, which is now a good code of practice for software developers attempting to acquire either ISO 9000 or BS 7750.

The way the testing and certification process works is well demonstrated by The Construction Products Directive, which sets out four alternative methods for the attestation of conformity, required by the CE Mark, which are:

1. Full third party certification of product conformity coupled with third party assessment and surveillance of factory production control.
2. Manufacturer's declaration of product conformity with third party assessment of factory production control.
3. Manufacturer's declaration of product conformity on the basis of third party initial type test, with manufacturer's declaration of factory product control.
4. Manufacturer's declaration of product conformity and factory production control.

It can be seen from the above that the attestation of conformity can be either through certification by an accreditation agency or declaration by the manufacturer.

This is a reminder that in the spirit of a free market a voluntary system of certification still exists in certain cases between supplier and customer. There are in fact eight 'modules' which are various ways of providing proof of conformity, one of which allows the manufacturer to take full responsibility and does not require a third party accreditation body. This, however, is a complex area for which space will not allow us further analysis and the reader should consult a local accreditation agency for advice on specific products. Even in a so called voluntary area of product certification, ISO 9000 may probably also be demanded.

US and Canadian readers will find that the all five of the major standards and testing agencies in North America now certify to ISO 9000. They will also be good sources of information on the EC procedures, but the very best source is an EC body itself. This is why the national standards authority of a small country, such as Ireland, the NSAI, has found that it can sell its ISO 9000 certification to international companies in the US and elsewhere overseas. Both ISO 9000 and information on the EC's certification requirements have become an export business from Europe.

The certification schemes associated with the EC Eco-scheme and BS 7750 were not defined at the time of writing. Each member state had to have a scheme in place by 1994, while the UK's Department of Trade and Industry, in its wisdom, was setting up a certification scheme for BS 7750, which should also satisfy the requirements of the Eco-scheme. The wisdom is in realizing how important the environment standard is for British exporters, and it places the UK's DTI, not the DoE, in the role of certification watchdog, as if it were saying that British industry and its exports need BS 7750 and this is the business of the DTI. Whether this position continues remains to be seen, but it is virtually certain that departments of the environment and especially environmental protection agencies (EPAs), elsewhere will want to administer this standard and how they do so may determine the success of whole economies. In the case of other European countries, allowing some of their departments of the environment to gain control of the environment certification scheme may put the country at a competitive disadvantage, so poor have the reputations been of some DoEs in these countries.

In its brochure advertising BS 7750, BSI has the following to say, 'It may help companies meet the criteria of the proposed EC Regulation'. It goes on:

> BS 7750 is consistent with the draft European Community regulation to set up a voluntary scheme on environmental auditing (the Eco-scheme). Use of the standard may be seen as a first step to meeting its requirements.

In a separate paragraph in the brochure, it reveals that ISO and CEN are working on the development of an international standard on environmental management systems. It is clear from this that BSI expects, or hopes, that BS 7750 will follow the success of BS 5750, and result in an ISO and EN standard.

The press release announcing the launch ventures into the area of accreditation, saying:

It does not specify expected levels of organizational performance, but rather specifies a standardised management system that is capable of independent assessment and verification. Accreditation of any certification scheme linked to the standard will be controlled by the Department of Trade and Industry (DTI), who have indicated that they will not accredit any scheme until the position of European initiatives is much clearer.

That position is now clear since the European Parliament passed the Eco-management and auditing scheme regulation.

The BSI newsletter accompanying the launch carried a joint statement from the DTI and DoE welcoming the standard and stating that it was essential that it be compatible with the EC Eco-scheme regulation. It added that the arrangements for accrediting the companies which offer certification to the standard would not be put in place until the European position was clear and 'the government is in a position to take decisions on the accreditation arrangements which will be required under the EC Eco-audit regulation'. (Since renamed Eco-Management and Auditing Scheme Regulation.)

At the time of writing, two other groups were becoming involved in certifying the certifiers. These were the Association of Certification Bodies (ACB) and the National Accreditation Council for Certification Bodies (NACCB). These, however, were trying to become the overseeing accreditation body for the UK, but in an open single market certified assessors and certification agencies may operate anywhere.

Also, at the time of writing, several private certification companies were offering to certify to BS 7750. Some of these were offering their own symbols to companies, which they had certified to the standard, and were expecting that these would get retrospective accreditation when the formal scheme came into being. There is opportunity here, however, for early achievers of the standard, for there is nothing to stop them declaring that they are operating to the standard once the systems it asks for are installed.

The complex subject of testing and certification is not made easier by the fact that it is changing at the time of writing as attempts are being made to harmonize practices within the new single market. Within the EC, the harmonization of testing and certification services is a natural follow-on to the process of harmonizing standards. Where a single standard, or set, is agreed, this can have practical consequences only if common certification schemes exist, and if each national scheme is accepted throughout Europe or internationally. As a number of US and

other overseas agencies are qualified to certify to the ISO 9000
standard, we can assume that any country whose agencies can certify
to ISO 9000 has the infrastructure to set up certification schemes
to certify to an environment standard, such as that demanded by the
Eco-scheme.

The steps needed to achieve the CE Mark, can be lengthy, time
consuming and highly technical. Here is an example of what one
company had to go through, based on the experiences of The Johnson
Manufacturing Company, which came to the west of Ireland from the
US, and is now Irish-owned. It needed the CE Mark both for the EC
automotive component market and for its pressure vessels. The steps
were as follows:

1. Membership of the EC technical committee which determines
   the specifications and standards for their product. This was
   crucial as each country's manufacturers seek to have the
   standard structured in such a way as to give them a competitive
   advantage. By being on the committee, one can influence the
   final product standard and, of course, learn from other manufacturer's presentations. By participating through this process, a
   company can both understand and influence the directives, and
   the requirements of supporting standards, as they are emerging.
   A single company can also represent its industry group and its
   country on a technical committee.
2. Implementing a project to bring about the changes needed within
   one's own company. This can involve product design, production processes, equipment and tooling, training needs, operator
   qualifications, material specification and certification, and any
   outside certification required.
3. Preparation of all the documentation required, from drawings
   to detailed specifications, controls, and management systems.
   Presentation of drawings for certification. Product drawings
   have to be certified prior to building samples for testing.
4. The construction of prototypes for submission to the certifying
   body for approval.
5. Implementation of the new product design, tooling, and so on,
   the production operations and implementation of the rigorous
   monitoring, testing and control procedures necessary to ensure
   continuing compliance. All of this is supplementary to the ISO
   9000 requirements which can only now be regarded as a starting
   point.

The cost to Johnson in achieving the CE Mark was in excess of £200,000 and two years of real commitment from top management, particularly the engineering personnel who have been given the major credit for the achievement. The payback has been very substantial, including access to vast European markets. Without the CE Mark they would have been excluded, as the requirement for the Mark is now mandatory for their product range.

Clearly a strong aggressive marketing campaign was also required to realize the potential opened up by the CE approval. Johnson also implemented a major marketing campaign to establish the company as dynamic, technically competent and innovative. This was particularly important as Johnson, being a relatively small engineering company based in the west of Ireland, would clearly be very difficult to sell to technically sophisticated EC buyers.

Hand in hand with implementing EC directives, is the related matter of obtaining quality approvals, which are the method of demonstrating continued compliance throughout the period of manufacture. Here are some relevant certification schemes, although readers should get specific details from their local certification agencies as to which products and markets all the various schemes refer.

Certification of the manufacturing facility can be obtained through:

- ISO-9001, EN29001.
- BABT 340.
- AQAP 4.

Most directives and standards also demand demonstrable or certified calibration and testing procedures. These may need the services of independent, usually government owned centres, such as a national metrology laboratory, a national electronics test centre, and a national accredited calibration and testing laboratory.

A national metrology laboratory maintains traceable standards in the fields of electricity, time and frequency, mass, force, pressure, temperature, volume and length. It maintains these measurement standards for a country and disseminates them to users within the country through its calibration service. It also offers traceability through the standards to international standards. Its services cover calibration in the following areas:

- Mass.
- Volume.

- Temperature.
- Pressure and force.
- Dimensional.
- Electrical.

A national electronics test centre may be the body listed in the EC *Official Journal* for functions such as electrical safety testing in accordance with the European Low Voltage Directive, while the centre's quality assurance engineers may provide an inspection service for electronic component manufacturers undergoing certification. If one wants to connect equipment to a European telecommunications network, for example, it can be tested by such a centre. Typical testing would cover:

- Telecoms.
- ISDN conformance.
- WAN terminal conformance.
- BUS conformance.
- Safety.

Typical approvals testing would apply to the following telecommunications devices:

- Facsimile machines.
- Telephones.
- PABX systems.
- Telephone answering machines.
- Modems.
- Payphones.
- Key telephone systems.

Dealing with these and other testing applications areas are the following services:

- Safety and environmental testing.
- Conformance testing.
- Electromagnetic compatibility testing (EMC).

Examples of devices and systems needing safety and environmental testing are:

- IT equipment.
- Telecoms.
- Measurement, control and laboratory equipment.
- Household electronics.
- Equipment connected to the telecom network.
- Plugs and sockets.

Very important bodies in Europe for manufacturers are the national accredited calibration and testing laboratories. These operate under the international body known as ILAC, the International Laboratory Accreditation Conference, which is an informal organization with no rules or regulations, but which has become a recognized international forum for accreditation. Many of its documents have become international guides through ISO and such European standards as EN 45000 dealing with accreditation. ILAC accreditation can be obtained by the accredited bodies within each country, and all the national laboratories under the ILAC label are accredited to operate to ILAC standards. ILAC certification is available to anyone involved in supplying testing, measurement and calibration facilities, within manufacturers or independently, government, private or educational. Each ILAC accredited laboratory has been assessed by skilled specialist assessors and found to meet ILAC criteria which in turn are structured on ISO/IEC guides and EN 45001.

There are four categories of laboratory A, B, C and D.

- Category A: permanent laboratory testing and calibration where the laboratory is erected on a fixed location for a period expected to be greater than three years.
- Category B: site testing and calibration that are performed by staff sent out on site by a permanent laboratory that is accredited by ILAC.
- Category C: site testing and calibration that are performed in a site/mobile laboratory or by staff sent out by such a laboratory, the operation of which is the responsibility of a permanent laboratory accredited by ILAC.
- Category D: site testing and calibration that are performed on site by individuals and organizations that do not have a permanent testing laboratory. Testing may be performed using: portable testing equipment, a site laboratory, a mobile laboratory, or equipment from a mobile or site laboratory.

Each national accredited laboratory refers back to ILAC. The ILAC accreditation criteria are in accordance with the recommendations of ISO Guide 25 and are the same as EN 45001. Size of laboratory is not a factor; competence is, as are quality of work and objectivity. Here are the criteria assessed:

- General organization and staff.
- Quality system.
- Testing and measuring equipment.
- Calibration.
- Test methods and procedures.
- Testing environment.
- Sample handling and identification.
- Recording of data.
- Reporting of results.

The implications of ILAC accreditation are fundamental for the single market. Until recently, only Greece and Luxembourg lacked national laboratory accreditation schemes. Greece is now setting up its own, while Luxembourg is using that of a neighbour's. In the wider world there are now forty national schemes developed to the same internationally agreed criteria. It can be seen that becoming, or setting up, an ILAC accredited laboratory could create business opportunities. It could also give rise to diversification possibilities for existing inhouse laboratories.

In 1989 the EC published a document titled *A Global Approach to Certification and Testing*. This was approved by a Council Resolution in 1989 stating, 'Member States should commit themselves to promoting the use of the EN 45000 series as widely as possible'. Accreditation by ILAC demonstrates that a laboratory meets the requirements of the EN 45000 series of standards.

CHAPTER 25

Other Supports Available to Small and Medium-sized Enterprises

The opportunities which now follow are also based on the analysis of EC grants and supports possibilities in the booklet published jointly by the international accounting and consulting firm KPMG and the Small Firms Association of the Confederation of Irish Industries. It is relevant to all SMEs across the Community. The title of the study is *EC Grants Guide – a comprehensive guide to EC grants and support programmes aimed at small and medium sized companies.*

BC-NET (Business Cooperation Network)

BC-NET is a computerized European network under the auspices of DG XXIII-B, which is responsible for measures in favour of small and medium-sized enterprises. BC-NET is complementary to BRE and Europartenariat. It was set up to make the process of finding a business partner in Europe much easier.

The aim of BC-NET is to encourage cooperation and partnership between like businesses in different regions of the community, enabling them to meet the challenge of the wider European market and compete against their large competitors. This is achieved by helping one company find another complementary company to cooperate in the areas of international finance, commerce and technical collaboration (including sharing of technologies and direct subcontracting), thus making EC small businesses more competitive in an increasingly competitive marketplace.

The network is formed of company advisors, who are true intermediaries subject to a professional code of conduct. The identification of potential partners is undertaken confidentially and rapidly. Company advisors can include private consultants, chambers of commerce, banks, business agencies, solicitors or regional development agencies. Codes are used to prepare the 'cooperation profile' on behalf of the SME and it will be sent to the Brussels central data-processing unit where it will be stored in the BC-NET databank and the request will be matched with coded offers stored in the databank. An immediate answer will be sent to the originator of the request and the originator of the offer if an appropriate match is made. If no match is made, the profile will be sent as a 'flash profile' to BC-NET users in the geographical area covered by the request.

When the ideal partner is found, the BC-NET advisors to the two potential partners are notified and they will make the initial contact and the first stage of negotiations. The identity of both partners will be revealed only on the approval of the SMEs involved.

BC-NET is an excellent tool to aid companies preparing to enter new markets. It assists SMEs by identifying distribution agencies in target areas, by providing access to new technology and expanding the company's field of production. BC-NET consists of a computerized network of over 600 consultants in the private and public sectors across Europe and worldwide. It covers all branches of industry and service and all types of commercial, technical and financial cooperation. Over 37,000 cooperation profiles have been handled by BC-NET since its inception in July 1988.

BIC (Business Innovation Centre)

There is a network of about 60 BICs being formed throughout Europe with the support of the European Commission. Financial support has been received from the European Regional Development Fund and from local private and public organizations.

The aim is to assist the economic regeneration by intensively and selectively supporting the development of new and established small businesses. The following range of services may be available:

- Practical support for entrepreneurs wishing to engage in start up activities or to develop the potential of an existing small business.
- Provision of advice and consultancy support in the following areas:
  (a) Business planning, market research and development.
  (b) Local/international technology search and assessment.
  (c) R&D, technology transfer and protection.
  (d) Legal, commercial and financial matters.
- Access to sources of seed and early stage venture capital.
- Provision or arrangement of facilities for R&D, shared work space and incubator units.
- Provision of ongoing assistance to projects and ventures during their early development phases.

After the selection phase, the BIC usually offers SMEs some kind of contractual arrangement whereby risk and success are shared. If the enterprise is successful the BIC is paid a fee. In the event of failure, it loses the time and advice it invested.

BICs concentrate on ventures operating or planning to locate in their area, and which are concerned with manufacturing, technology related services and other innovative activities. Clients should have the potential to create employment and to become exporters. BIC clients are likely to be drawn from the following groups:

- Entrepreneurs, innovators with specific projects in mind.
- Experienced managers or technologists interested in joining BIC supported ventures.
- Established small businesses with sound bases for further innovative development.

Many BIC projects are likely to involve the commercial exploitation of new technologies within specific market niches where competitive advantages could be acquired and sustained. BIC is particularly interested in clients referred to it by professional advisors, industrial,

financial and educational institutions, state agencies and local employment and enterprise organizations.

BRE (Bureau de Rapprochement des Enterprises)

BRE has been operational since 1973. Set up by the Commission to
assist SMEs to find partners beyond their national frontiers. The aim is
to promote cross-border cooperation on a non-confidential basis. It
operates through a network of correspondents located in all member
states. The network enables SMEs to look for partners in other regions,
publicises the cooperation opportunities proposed by companies in
other countries and advises SMEs in the negotiation of cooperation
agreements.

Similar in operation to BS-NET, it has a wider geographical coverage
as it operates in 32 non-member countries as well as the 12 member
countries. The BRE service is currently operated free of charge to SMEs.
A fee many be introduced in the future.

BRITE/EURAM II – Specific training

BRITE/EURAM II exists to train technologists for European industry.
   Grant assistance:

- Grants may be available to ongoing project consortia to engage
  research scientists and experts (marketing, norms and standards,
  production management, technology transfer specialists) to
  assist in working on specific BRITE/EURAM projects and
  promoting the research results. Eligible costs may include
  research, mobility and labour costs.
- Grants may also be available towards the costs of courses and
  conferences relevant to the BRITE/EURAM programme and
  aimed at researchers, scientists, industrialists and others needing to be trained to perform specific tasks linked with industrial
  R&D and exploitation of results.
- Industrial Research Fellowships.

Duration: 3–36 months. EC contribution: negotiated with the Commission.

COMETT II (Community Action Programme in Education and Training for Technology)

COMETT II exists to promote cooperation between universities and industry in the field of training for advanced technology, to meet the requirements of companies, and in particular SMEs, for qualified personnel, and to set up transnational networks for technology training projects.

Duration: 1990–1994. EC contribution: ECU 200 million. Grant assistance: Grants of up 50 per cent of eligible expenditure up to a maximum of ECU 50,000 for University Enterprise Training Partnerships (UETPS). These can be organized on a sectoral basis, such as timber and wood processing industries or on a regional basis.

UETPS can then apply for grant assistance for the following:

- Grants of up to ECU 6000 per year per student undertaking 3–12 months training in industry in another member country.
- Grants of up to ECU 15,000 for personnel seconded for 3 month periods from university to industry or vice versa in another member country.
- Grants of up to ECU 30,000 for training courses within a European context in new technologies and their applications.

Project eligibility: University/industry cooperative projects involving partners from at least two member states in the production of advanced training packages in technological areas not readily available elsewhere and which are produced on a European basis, for example lasers and optoelectronics, information technology for SMEs, tourism. University is defined as public authorities, financial and insurance institutions, chambers of commerce, industry federations, employee and employer representative organizations.

Many of the courses are technology led, however, it is possible that industry groups can identify areas where they require technology training and can approach educational institutions to pursue the possibility of a submission under COMETT.

The main beneficiaries are universities, college and training institutes in both the public and private sector. Employees of SMEs, such as company technicians, and engineers in management posts, benefit indirectly through access to the training course. Students in higher education and university graduates also benefit.

COST (European Cooperation in the Field of Scientific and Technical Research)

COST was established in 1971 to encourage cooperation in all areas of research. It is an association of member states as well as a host of other 'third' countries. COST projects aim at coordinating research problems, either existing or proposed, that tackle international problems. They promote the creation of scientific networks.

Duration: Ongoing. EC contribution: the budget is decided annually at around ECU 7 million. Grant assistance: COST differs from other EC programmes in that projects are not funded. The commission only covers up to 50–100 per cent of the coordination costs of ongoing research. Costs covered are secretarial assistance, translation facilities, workshop costs and some travel expenses. Project eligibility: the projects concentrate mainly on pre-competitive research and complement EC activities. There have to be at least four member countries participating before funding is considered. For example, projects to date have covered:

- Informatics.
- Telecommunications.
- Agriculture.
- Food technology.

EEIG (The European Economic Interest Grouping)

The EEIG was set up on 25 July 1989 under Regulation No: 2137/85 to encourage cross-border cooperation between EC companies in general and SMEs in particular, leading to joint activities in research and development, marketing, purchasing, distribution, coproduction, sales, computerized data processing and the formation of multidisciplinary consortia to tender for public and private contracts. The EEIGs are governed by Community legislation.

The EEIG is a legal instrument for transnational cooperation. Under the EEIG any form of economic activity is conceivable. It is a flexible form of association that allows its members to cooperate for the realization of a specific project, while at the same time retaining their economic and legal independence in the management of their own affairs.

Financing: the EEIG does not have to have its own capital on formation. It is up to the members themselves to decide how their grouping is to be financed. Contributions may be made in cash, kind or skills. They may decide to fund the grouping by annual subscription or by cash injections by each member from time to time. This programme is of major interest to SMEs who wish to trade in other EC member states.

EFEC (European Financial Engineering Company)

EFEC is responsible for engaging in all forms of financial engineering and, in particular, acts in an advisory capacity studying financing plans and promoting business ventures, with the emphasis on SMEs. The company will also provide integrated financial services for European enterprises investing in developing countries or counties in the Mediterranean region which have cooperation agreements with the EC.

Assistance:

- Raising of capital – venture capital development, banks and loan finance.
- Business development – establishments abroad, negotiations with regional, national and EC authorities, identification of industrial/commercial partners, organization of mergers/ acquisitions.
- Consultancy assignments – financial, economic, legal and tax related.

EIB (European Investment Bank)

The EIB contributes on a non-profit making basis to economic development through the provision of long-term loans for public and private capital investment in industry, energy and infrastructure and to foster the investment projects of SMEs.

Financial assistance: may be provided for large projects by direct loans or through other banks and for smaller projects through global loans provided by other banks.

Direct loans for large projects: loans of up to 50 per cent of a project's fixed asset cost up to certain limits may be available. Interest is at fixed or floating rates just over the EIBs cost of borrowing and repayments are made on a half-yearly basis.

Term loans of 4–12 years may be available for fixed asset projects in:

- Industry – manufacturing, processing, packaging, factory buildings and estates, quarrying and mining.
- Tourism.
- Forestry.
- Services related to tourism and industry.

Term loans of up to 20 years may be available for:

- Oil and gas developments.
- Infrastructure – telecommunications, water service, energy, roads, other transport.
- Environmental protection.

All EIB financing requires guarantees from one of the following: the government of the country in which the project is to take place, a first class bank, a banking syndicate, a financial grouping or a large internationally diversified parent company with a first class credit rating.

Application procedure: promoters may either submit their projects directly to EIB or may approach EIB through their own bank.

Global loans for small and medium-sized projects: loans of up to 50 per cent of project investment cost where the minimum project cost is approximately ECU 20,000 and the maximum is ECU 10 million. Term loans of 5–12 years. An exception of 15 years is made for new hotel development. Capital repayments can be made after several years. (Note: in general the advantage to a client is that medium-term fixed rate loans are available in a broad range of currencies at a fixed rate of funds which can be more attractive than would normally be available in the general market.) Project eligibility: new fixed asset projects in industry, tourism and related services.

The promoter must have net fixed assets, as shown on the balance sheet, of up to ECU 75 million, and employ up to 500 people before the project is carried out. Security and interest rates are negotiated with the intermediary bank whose criteria must also be met.

Application procedure for global loans: projects submitted to the intermediary financial institution are presented to EIB which then decides on one's eligibility. Beneficiaries: authorities, companies or consortia in public and private sectors.

ETP (Executive Training Programme)

A training programme for young managers from European Community-based companies to learn the Japanese language and gain work experience in Japan. The course lasts 18 months – a 12-month intensive language course followed by seminars and factory visits and 6 months inhouse training in selected Japanese companies.

The aim is to provide export-oriented executives with a knowledge of the Japanese language and marketplace.

Duration: indefinite. EC contribution: financial assistance for approximately 45 places. Language course and expenses linked to the programme are paid by the EC. Participants receive a monthly allowance and relocation expenses for moving to Japan and back again at the end of the programme. Eligibility: this course is aimed at European executives with university level education (or relevant professional experience) with a least two years work experience, employed in an export oriented EC company which has a particular project to export to Japan.

Candidates are either marketing specialists or general managers, but candidates with technical or scientific backgrounds will also be considered. Sponsoring companies must sign a declaration stating that they will continue to employ the participant during the training course and afterwards in Japan or possibly in Europe with a responsibility for Japan.

Europartenariat

This is dealt with in Chapter 10.

Eurotech capital

An initiative designed to encourage private companies to invest in and provide finance for the promoters of transnational high technology projects and for the SMEs taking part in them. The programme is aimed at promoting private financing of transnational projects through private organizations known as Eurotech funds. The organizations will be required to devote a specified amount of their capital to new venture capital financing of high technology projects. In return they will receive a financial contribution from the Commission and various other advantages, such as access to databases, organization of meetings between transnational high technology project promoters and Eurotech capital managers.

Duration: pilot project. EC contribution: a network at present comprising nine European venture capital companies has undertaken to invest a total of approximately EC 150 million. Project eligibility:

- High technology projects must:
  - (a) come under a Community research or development programme (EUREKA, VALUE, SPRINT, BRITE etc.),
  - (b) come under a national research programme, or,
  - (c) constitute a significant advance on existing technology.
- Transnational projects must:
  - (a) come under a Community or European research programme (EUREKA, VALUE, SPRINT, BRITE etc.), or
  - (b) have a research phase and an industrial applications phase in two or more countries, or have shareholders from two or more countries.
- Companies assisted are seed and start up companies and companies with fewer than 500 employees, fixed assets of not more than ECU 75 million and with not more than one third of capital held by large companies.

Beneficiaries: SMEs. Application procedure: under this action, services have been developed, one of which, Eurotech Invest, is particularly relevant to companies. A project identification service is available free of charge to any European firm wishing to attract investment by venture capital companies.

EUROTECHNET II (Programme in the Field of Vocational Training and Technological Change)

EUROTECHNET II is aimed at assessing the impact of technological changes on training requirements in order to develop new skills and qualifications.

Duration: 1990–1994. EC contribution: ECU 29 million.

**FORCE (Community Action Programme for the
Development of Continuing Vocational Training)**

FORCE is aimed at improving the supply and quality of vocational training for employees in companies. The programme has been designed for companies and associations who see training as a means of improving their competitive edge in the marketplace.

Duration: July 1991–December 1994. EC contribution: ECU 24 million for the first two years. This fund had just been increased at the time of publication, with new calls for proposals.

**INTERPRISE (Initiative to Encourage Partnerships among
Industries or Services in Europe)**

A separate and autonomous programme based on the successful format of the Europartenariat programme. It was set up to encourage cooperation and partnership arrangements between business and service companies in Europe. It supports local, regional and national actions targeted to stimulate contacts between entrepreneurs and cooperation and partnerships between SMEs. Programmes should involve a minimum of 3 regions of 3 different member states.

Project eligibility: projects should include the following stages:

- Identification and selection of businesses in the regions concerned which are interested in setting up a cooperation agreement with a company in one of the other participating regions.
- An active search for interested enterprises in regions concerned.
- Organizing a meeting, trade fair or conference, enabling direct contacts between interested companies in participating regions.

IRIS

IRIS was launched in 1988 and now has a membership of 450. Its objective is to build up a network of innovative projects to support and stimulate vocational training programmes to meet women's needs. The aims of the programme are to:

- Improve access for women to vocational training.
- Build links between women's training programmes throughout the EC.
- Create training methods specially adapted to women's needs.
- Increase involvement of employers and trade unions in vocational training programmes for women.
- Assist women to enter or re-enter the labour market.
- Improve women's qualifications.
- Help women to obtain a career promotion.

Duration: indefinite. EC contribution: ECU 500,000 annually. Grant assistance: funding is provided for exchange visits between projects involved in the network. Seminars are organized and funded as are any means to promote dissemination of information. For project eligibility training must:

- Encourage access to employment for women.
- Meet the demands of the local and regional labour markets.
- Use innovative teaching methods.
- Involve participants from employers, trade unions, employment/training agencies and public authorities.

Women's vocational training programmes can become members of the IRIS network free of charge. Once a part of the network, groups can apply for various grants. Beneficiaries: women's training projects, women.

Life sciences and technologies for developing countries

This programme aims to pool member state and developing countries R&D and to maximize the benefits to the latter.
   Duration: 1991–1994. EC contribution: ECU 111 million. (See also Chapter 9 under the above heading.)

**LINGUA (Community Action Programme to Promote
Foreign Language Competence in the European
Community)**

This programme seeks to improve the teaching and learning of foreign languages in education, training and working life.
   Duration: 1990–1994. EC contribution: ECU 200 million.

New venture consort scheme

This programme aims to encourage the formation of cross-border syndicates of venture capital companies investing in SMEs in all industrial and service sectors.

Duration: the scheme has recently being reviewed and will continue to operate in the immediate future. EC contribution: since its launch in 1988, 31 projects have been approved, resulting in a contribution of ECU 5.5 million. Grant assistance:

- Fixed sum, non-refundable contributions to a venture capital company which has identified a particular potential investee company to assist in meeting the expenses incurred:
  (a) In searching for other venture capital companies to establish a new transnational syndicate to invest in that investee company, the amount of the contribution up to ECU 3,000, and
  (b) successfully completing the financing of the SME investee company, the amount of contribution is up to either ECU 5,000 or ECU 10,000, depending on whether the new transnational syndicate consists of members from only two or more EC member states.
- A refundable advance of up to the lesser of 30 per cent or ECU 300,000 of syndicated equity investment may be provided by the Commission. An agreed mechanism applies whereby the EC can be bought out by the shareholder, that is, the venture capital companies and/or the investee company.
- The Commission is also currently examining the development of accompanying measures which would further support the development of new transnational syndications.

Project eligibility:

- Must involve SMEs.
- Innovative projects.
- Expansion into more than one member state.
- Financed by cross-border syndicate of venture capitalists who are members of the European Venture Capital Association.
- Coherence with other policies and programmes of the European Commission.

Beneficiaries: venture capital companies and investee companies situated in the EC, who have an innovative product and who are in discussion with a venture capital company in the local member state and can bring on board a venture capital company from another state may be eligible for some financial assistance. Contact: European Venture Capital Association, Keibergpark, Minervastratt 6, B-1930 Zaventem.

Scheme of grants for small and community enterprises

This scheme is supported by the EC's European Regional Development Fund to encourage initiative and support small enterprises in rural areas and keep people in rural areas by creating additional income.

For eligibility projects must:

- Be rurally based.
- Have potential for commercial viability.
- Create sustainable employment whether full time or seasonal.
- Be properly researched and funded.
- Not be eligible under any other existing grant structure.

The scheme will not be used to support investment in any primary agricultural production.

Seed capital funds

Twenty-four seed capital funds have been set up throughout the Community following the Commission's calls for proposals and they form part of a ESCF (European Seed Capital Fund Network) aimed at supporting business start-ups all over the Community. The network has ongoing contact with the EBN (European Business and Innovations Centre Network). Its purpose is to give financial support for seed capital funds designed to provide investment in the form of an equity participation in new or embryonic SMEs whose projects can promote development and innovation.

Duration: 1988–1993. EC contribution: ESCF has resources of some ECU 35 million. Grant assistance for SMEs. (Typical seed investments are likely to be in the range of ECU 25,000–100,000.) Project eligibility:

- Funds are committed to invest exclusively in the creation or development of enterprises which need management and financial support prior to turning to more traditional financial sources.
- Projects generally have a long development phase often involving new technology.
- External seed capital requirements of not more than ECU 350,000.
- The existing business must be a separate entity and meet the following conditions.
  (a) Existing risk capital investment of no more than ECU 50,000.
  (b) Annual sales less than ECU 100,000.
  (c) Less than 10 employees.
  (d) Total share capital not more than ECU 150,000.

Application procedure: contact the nearest seed capital fund. The project is then evaluated and the financing decision is taken solely by the fund. Beneficiaries: SMEs.

SPEC (Support Programme for Employment Creation)

SPEC aims to provide financial support and technical assistance to local job creation projects, particularly in less developed regions. This programme also attempts to improve awareness, experiment with and test innovative ideas for job creation.

Duration: Reviewed on an annual basis. EC contribution: decided annually – around ECU 900,000.

TED (Tenders Electronic Daily)

Online directory of invitations to tender for public works and supply contracts covering EC member states and for Africa, the Caribbean and Pacific countries associated with the EC. It also covers non-associated countries carrying out projects financed by the European Development Fund and under GATT from Sweden, Japan and the USA.

TED is the online version of the Supplement (S Series) to the *Official Journal of the European Communities*. The documents are available on the morning of their publication. Documents dealing with areas of special interest can be directly accessed by means of subject and country codes.

Languages: all official languages of the EC except Greek. Costs are ECU 42 per connect hour. Access: European Business Information Centre.

This is a most important service for those selling into the EC public procurement market. See Chapters 5, 6, 7 and 8.

EAGGF (The European Agricultural Guidance and Guarantee Fund)

EAGGF aims to modernize, diversify and develop agricultural and forestry structures, maintain landscape and develop rural areas.

CHAPTER 26

Banking Facilities

The material in this chapter was kindly supplied by the International Services Office of Barclays Bank plc.

A good bank with an international department will assist trade in the internal market, and between companies within the internal market and overseas, by offering facilities which cover all aspects of foreign trade, from currency exchange services and market information to payment methods, documentation and export finance.

A good bank can also assist in the management of exchange rate risks and credit risks, with a choice of facilities that can help one achieve certainty of payment and even help to collect money owed. International services specialists, such as those at Barclays, can help one make informed decisions, control terms of trading, save administration time, reduce uncertainty and generally enhance one's competitive position wherever one wishes to trade.

Barclays publishes a booklet entitled *International Trade Services*, from which the broad range of international trade services in banking has been drawn together and displayed in Table 26.1 and which are discussed in the following sections.

TABLE 26.1

Service	Ideal for
Trade development service Trading information for both importers and exporters.	Businesses seeking trading partners abroad.
Economic information service Economic information on the world's major trading areas.	Businesses wishing to make informed decisions based on accurate and timely information.
Foreign currency accounts Current and deposit accounts in every major foreign currency.	Businesses wishing to reduce exchange risk by maintaining foreign currency accounts.
International money transfer services A wide range of services for varying money transfer requirements.	All businesses needing to pay overseas suppliers or receive payments from overseas customers.
Export finance A range of lending services designed to help businesses trading abroad.	Businesses requiring short term finance for extra working capital.
Exchange rate services Foreign exchange risk management for exporters and importers.	Any business invoicing or being invoiced in a foreign currency.
Reducing risk of non-payment in international trade Ways to send and receive international payments.	Exporters or importers seeking to reduce international trading risks.

Trade development service

This is an information and database service bringing buyers and suppliers together. The service combines information and database services to help identify and link thousands of potential customers and suppliers worldwide. The global resources offered by the service are available to any size and type of business, whether importing or exporting. If, for example, one uses Barclays for this service, one does not have to be an existing Barclays customer.

One may also place details of one's business onto a worldwide trade-opportunity database, which gives easy access to the vast international marketplace, 24 hours a day, 365 days a year. Through a database, such as Barclays 'Business', the bank can formulate a search strategy that will enable a company to pinpoint trading partners to match the requirements of its particular business. In turn, the business may also advertise to thousands of interested companies the world over.

Economic information service

Such a service helps companies to trade abroad simply by being better informed.

If a company has limited time and resources, there may be numerous sources of business information currently unknown to it. In such a case, whether it is an exporter or an importer, a comprehensive economic information service may help it increase trading profits by being more closely aware of worldwide economic developments.

The economic information service can provide a company with information and analyses on interest rates, exchange rates, industries, commodities and countries, either through individually commissioned research or through a bank's business publications.

The business publications will embrace the findings of a wide range of periodicals covering financial and economic trends, both at home and overseas, including assessments of economic prospects in the major developing countries and eastern Europe.

Currency guides and reports will deal with key currencies and interest rates, as well as selected secondary and exotic currencies.

Foreign currency accounts

When one trades abroad, one may be paying and receiving money in a foreign currency. It may therefore make sound business sense to open a foreign currency current account. Such an account will save a company both time and the administrative cost of converting the foreign currency funds into local funds and back again as well as avoiding the risk of exchange rate fluctuations. Foreign currency payments received can be credited directly into the account, allowing immediate access to these funds via a cheque book or inter-bank transfer.

Raising finance through a foreign currency current account is simple and convenient. Subject to status, one can apply to borrow by either overdraft or loan. Borrowing in a foreign currency helps protect oneself against foreign exchange risks when selling in that currency. An overdraft or loan can be repaid from payments received from customers, in the same currency, avoiding the effects of exchange rate fluctuations.

Surplus funds accumulating in foreign currency accounts and not required immediately can be made to work in interest-earning foreign currency deposit accounts. Barclays, for example, offers two types of foreign currency deposit account for any currency freely traded in London.

Call Deposit Accounts give same-day access to funds held in US or Canadian dollars, and two-day access to all other currencies. With call deposit accounts, interest is earned on cash surplusses as low as US$2,000, or its equivalent in any other currency. One may also earn interest at higher rates on minimum balances of US$10,000, or the equivalent, in *Fixed Deposit Accounts*. These accounts pay interest on maturity or on each anniversary of the investment. These dollar figures are, of course, subject to exchange rate fluctuations and are subject to change.

International money transfer services

Moving money around the world is an essential requirement in international trade, which is why good international banks offer importers and exporters a variety of money transfer services to suit differing business requirements in terms of speed, security and cost. Each method offers a convenient way to transfer funds from the home base to any named individual overseas or to receive funds from abroad. The leading banks' international money transfer services are available through any of their branches and, in most cases, through correspondent banks overseas.

The transfer method chosen will depend largely on how much money one wishes to send and how urgently it is required. For larger amounts in any major currency, an *International Payment Order* is the ideal method of electronic funds transfer. If it is desired to enclose supporting documents with the payment, however, one may arrange to have the international payment order sent by mail.

For urgent payments, the fastest way to transfer funds abroad is by *Telegraphic Transfer*, an electronic bank-to-bank payments method which gives security of delivery.

Export finance

Whenever it is necessary to obtain funds on a short-term basis to finance large export orders, or to service important contracts, or to trade abroad, there are a number of ways to help raise the extra working capital required.

For smaller companies with an annual export turnover of less than £2 million, Barclays has a scheme called 'Tradeflow' to help enhance their competitive position. When exporting goods, this scheme can provide, on proof of export, 100 per cent of the value of the invoice. By having the funds immediately available, one may be able to enhance one's competitive position with overseas customers by granting them more credit or through other arrangements. Such a smaller exports scheme allows companies to extend credit directly to customers and the bank's involvement is not revealed. Customers therefore see the company, and not the bank, as the provider of credit. The company also has the added protection of a bank's own credit insurance, covering any loss to the business if the customer defaults on payment, or becomes insolvent. Customers must be approved by the bank, and because all insurance administration and paperwork are handled by the bank, valuable business time is saved.

Cash advances through a smaller exports scheme can be made available in any acceptable foreign currency. This reduces trading risks still further in that it minimizes exposure to adverse changes in exchange rates.

A second method of using export finance is *International Factoring*. This provides an immediate answer to the cash flow problems often created by slow payments, which can threaten the success of an export deal. International factoring immediately releases money tied up in a sales ledger and with cash made available in this way, a company can make purchases in bulk to take advantage of discounts from suppliers. It may also accept large orders and offer customers more flexible credit terms.

In most circumstances, international factoring can provide full credit cover against bad debts. One hundred per cent payment of invoices (less charges) can be guaranteed whether customers eventually pay or not.

International factoring may also save time and administration costs by supporting companies with a credit checking and management service if required. If one has a projected annual turnover of £200,000 or more in sales over the next 12 months and operates on credit terms which are accepted in one's industry, full advantage of such a service can be taken.

Exchange rate services

All currencies are vulnerable to the many factors that affect exchange rates. Like other goods or commodities, their prices are influenced by the market forces of supply and demand. Therefore, whether in import or export, one is inevitably exposed to some form of exchange rate risk. A leading international bank can offer a variety of exchange rate services to manage and mitigate such risks, whatever the size and nature of the business.

Through a *Forward Exchange Transaction,* one enters into a binding agreement to exchange, at a date in the future, a specified amount of one currency for another at a rate agreed now. This fixes the exchange rate which will be used to settle future import or export payments relieving uncertainty and allowing accurate calculation of costs. A bank will offer to forward exchange contracts in many currencies to complement the immediate 'spot' cover available in such currencies. Payments arising from a 'spot' transaction are settled in the currencies involved two working days after the date of dealing.

A *Currency Option* gives the right, but not the obligation, to buy or sell a given amount of one currency against another at a pre-agreed price on a single date in the future, or between the date the contract is agreed and its expiry date. Having bought a currency option, one combines the certainty of having fixed the exchange with the flexibility of being able to benefit from favourable exchange rate movements, since one is not obliged to take up the option. Options are an excellent solution if one requires a particular amount of a foreign currency at some future date which cannot yet be determined and are a good way of 'hedging' against the uncertainties of currency movements.

Letters of credit

Letters of Credit reduce the risk of non-payment in international trade.

Whether one is importing or exporting, a letter of credit is the most effective method of safeguarding one's international trade. A letter of credit is issued by the importer's bank and is a written undertaking on the importer's behalf. It provides for payment immediately on presentation of shipping documents or within a specified number of days.

As an exporter, one knows in advance that one will be paid on a specified date, so cash flow can be accurately predicted. Better credit terms may be offered to customers. Letters of credit, confirmed by a reputable bank, are ideal for larger payments or when maximum security and control are required and give the assurance of guaranteed payments, provided all the terms and conditions cited in the letter of credit are met.

If one is an importer, the letter of credit is one of the best ways to reduce international trading risks. With a letter of credit, one may specify exactly when and under what conditions payment will be made, who will pay transport costs, and when and how goods are to be shipped. Only when suppliers have met all these conditions will they be paid. Also, because suppliers are assured of payment of a specified amount at a specified time, one is in an ideal position to negotiate larger discounts over longer credit periods.

Another safeguard is an *International Collection*, which, for shipments by sea, enables the supplier to retain control of the goods exported until the buyer pays with cleared funds, which are immediately credited to the supplier's account. In this way, the international collection ensures that customers do not obtain possession of the goods before payment is made. All the shipping documents are sent by the bank to the importer's bank where they are released to the importer upon payment.

APPENDIX 1

Sample Life-of-programme Agreement

Amdahl has very generously allowed us to reproduce its life-of-programme agreement which governs supplier conditions for its European manufacturing facility near Dublin.

LIFE OF PROGRAM AGREEMENT

AGREEMENT NUMBER XXX

This Agreement is entered into this (DATE), between Amdahl Ireland Limited, Balheary, Swords, Co. Dublin, herein after referred to as 'AMDAHL' or 'CUSTOMER', and _____, of _____, herein after referred to as 'SUPPLIER'.

1. Agreement

The provisions of this agreement, including all Supplements and Schedules, constitute the entire agreement between both parties and supersede all prior agreements relating to the subjects contained herein. No amendment, modification or supplement may be made to this Agreement without its inclusion in this Agreement and must be agreed to and signed by both parties.

2. Term of agreement

(A) The Initial Term of this Agreement shall be for a period commencing 1st. July 1991, and ending with the ceasing of the manufacture by CUSTOMER of the 5995M system, or any immediate derivative thereof, unless terminated as provided herein.

(B) After the Initial Term, this Agreement may be renewed for a further agreed period, as business need dictates. Such renewal shall be accomplished by CUSTOMER giving written notice of renewal at least ninety (90) days prior to expiry of the Initial Term of this Agreement.

(C) Orders, forecasts or firmed requirements issued prior to termination of the Agreement shall survive such termination.

3. Contract

The following documents together with this Agreement form the Contract and are fully part of the Contract:

Individual Purchase Orders and Forecasts referencing this Agreement Number together with the following Attachments:

Supplement 1: Purchase Order Terms and Conditions.
Schedule 1:   Product Definition, Pricing, Amdahl-owned Tooling, Rescheduling and Cancellation Criteria.

4. Purchase order terms and conditions

Any printed Terms and Conditions on individual Purchase Orders or

Forecasts shall be superseded by this Agreement and Supplement 1 where the Purchase Order or the Forecast Terms are inconsistent.

5. Pricing

Pricing for all units ordered shall be at the prices listed in Schedule 1. CUSTOMER and the SUPPLIER will review prices, lead-times and other terms together at three monthly intervals. Any revised pricing will prevail from the first delivery after the agreed implementation date.

6. Forecasts and ordering

CUSTOMER will issue to the SUPPLIER a Forecast of estimated requirements by Product for the next 12 month period. Forecasts will be updated on a monthly basis. This will be a good faith estimate of projected usage for the next 12 months.

CUSTOMER may reschedule units according to Schedule 1 of this Agreement.

The SUPPLIER is required to return the acceptance portion of the Forecast document as an indication of his agreement or otherwise with the delivery requirements thereof within 5 days of receipt.

7. Quantity

CUSTOMER agrees to purchase its normal production requirements of the part number(s) described in Schedule 1 from the SUPPLIER over the term of this Agreement provided that the SUPPLIER:

- meets the delivery requirements set out in the forecasts;
- meets the quality standards as defined in the product specification;
- enters into a mutually satisfactory price agreement with CUSTOMER; and
- agrees to permit CUSTOMER to reasonably adjust its purchases to take account of exceptional or inter-company requirements, which permission will not be unreasonably withheld.

8. Termination for cause

If CUSTOMER reasonably determines that the SUPPLIER is unable to conform to the requirements of this Agreement, CUSTOMER may terminate the Agreement upon seven days written notice for cause, should all other avenues of redress have failed to remove the cause. In all cases, the SUPPLIER shall be given sixty (60) days prior written notice of any alleged default under this agreement within which time such alleged default must be cured or corrected.

Termination for cause shall include, but not be limited to, the following:

- serious breach by the SUPPLIER of any term or condition of this Agreement;
- an assignment by the SUPPLIER for the benefit of its creditors;
- an admission by the SUPPLIER of its inability to pay debts;
- the appointment of a Receiver, Liquidator or Examiner to the SUPPLIER;
- the failure to provide reasonable assurances of future performance acceptable to CUSTOMER.

In the event of termination for cause, CUSTOMER shall not be liable to the SUPPLIER for any amount other than in respect of material already received by Amdahl.

9. Cancellation

In the event of cancellation of all outstanding forecasted requirements, CUSTOMER will be responsible for mutually agreed maximum quantities of material (including work done on such material) as laid down in Schedule 1, provided such quantities are consistent with the materials and process lead times, and the forecast supplied by CUSTOMER.

10. Cost effectiveness

CUSTOMER is relying upon the SUPPLIER'S expertise to ensure compliance with CUSTOMER'S specifications to maximize cost effectiveness, quality and reliability of units supplied. The SUPPLIER recognizes that the benefits of the Life of Program Agreement allow him to concentrate his efforts on strengthening the business, improving quality and reducing manufacturing costs.

The SUPPLIER is expected to provide technical support and value analysis/value engineering support for quality and cost improvement and will, over the period of the Agreement make every reasonable effort to reduce the sales price of the items listed in Schedule 1 per the review periods agreed in Clause 5 above.

11. Specification

Units supplied will be produced to comply with CUSTOMER'S specification and quality standards which the SUPPLIER has read and accepts. No substitution of materials or change in process or standards shall be permitted on units unless previously agreed to in writing by CUSTOMER.

12. Delivery

The SUPPLIER agrees to deliver exact quantities as specified on Purchase Orders or Forecasts. SUPPLIER agrees to deliver units to CUSTOMER'S designated point of destination on the acknowledged due date. Any late delivery shall be priority shipped, on request by CUSTOMER and per CUSTOMER'S instructions. No extra charge shall be incurred by CUSTOMER in connection with expediting late deliveries.

13. ISO 9000 and quality systems

The SUPPLIER will achieve and maintain approval of its Quality System in accordance with ISO 9000, the internationally recognised Quality System Standard, throughout the life of this Agreement. At the commencement of supply of product to CUSTOMER, the SUPPLIER will agree and document the manufacturing process for each product item and will not alter or deviate from this process without consultation with and agreement in writing from a CUSTOMER technical representative. CUSTOMER will at all times have access to relevant quality information. A schedule of System and Process audits will be agreed with the SUPPLIER as part of this Agreement, at which process and quality information will be exchanged, discussed and analysed. The SUPPLIER agrees to maintain full quality records of his process as laid down in his manufacturing process documents.

14. Accounts

The SUPPLIER agrees to submit, to designated CUSTOMER personnel, copies of its quarterly management accounts and annual audited accounts for review. CUSTOMER will treat such accounts as strictly confidential.

15. Confidentiality

The SUPPLIER agrees to treat all information received from CUSTOMER with the strictest confidence and to use such information solely for the purposes of conducting its relations with CUSTOMER as laid down in Supplement 1 attached.

16. Arbitration

All differences and disputes between the parties shall be submitted to arbitration by a sole arbitrator, to be appointed (in the absence of agreement between the parties upon such appointment and on the application of either of them) by the President for the time being of the Confederation of Irish Industry, such arbitration to be governed by the Arbitration Acts of 1954 and 1980.

17. Signed

On behalf of AMDAHL: On behalf of the SUPPLIER:

_____ Date _____   _____
(CHIEF EXECUTIVE)   (NAME OF COMPANY)

_____ Date _____   _____

(DIR. FINANCE)   (NAME – BLOCK LETTERS)

_____ Date _____   _____ Date _____

(DIR. MATERIALS)   (SIGNATURE)

Title _____

LIFE OF PROGRAMME AGREEMENT NUMBER 015

SUPPLEMENT 1

TERMS AND CONDITIONS

1. Acceptance

The signing of this Life of Program Agreement by the SUPPLIER shall constitute SUPPLIER'S unconditional and irrevocable acceptance of all the Agreement's Terms and Conditions and shall take effect immediately on its receipt at CUSTOMER.

Any term or condition proposed by SUPPLIER whether before or after SUPPLIER'S receipt of this Agreement and whether purporting to form part of or to be communicated to CUSTOMER with the said signed copy Agreement or otherwise shall be null and void and of no effect for any purpose whatsoever unless the same shall have been agreed to by CUSTOMER and expressed in writing and signed by the duly authorised representatives of both the parties hereto.

2. Packing and transport

(A) All shipments shall be packed in accordance with CUSTOMER'S specifications or, if none are specified, in accordance with standard commercial practice. All shipments will be so packed as to prevent damage in transit, assure lowest transport cost and meet carrier's tariff requirements. No charge to CUSTOMER shall be made for boxing, crating or storage without its prior written authorization. Each shipping container shall be clearly marked to indicate the applicable Delivery Reference Number, CUSTOMER Part Number and quantity.

(B) Transportation instructions may be given to SUPPLIER. In this case, SUPPLIER shall not deviate from them without CUSTOMER'S prior written consent. If no transport instructions are provided, SUPPLIER shall transport goods to assure lowest transport costs while meeting carrier's tariff requirements.

3. Shipping; delivery; risk of loss

(A) SUPPLIER shall deliver goods and services in accordance with the Forecast supplied by CUSTOMER. The Forecast states the date on which the material is due at the designated point of delivery. Time is of the essence.

(B) Without CUSTOMER'S prior written permission, the SUPPLIER shall not ship goods to be received by CUSTOMER more than two (2) days in advance of Forecast due date or zero days late.

(C) SUPPLIER shall notify CUSTOMER immediately when it is known that there is a potential for a delay in delivery.

(D) SUPPLIER shall deliver the exact quantities set out in the Forecast. CUSTOMER reserves the right to reject over-shipments and return them to the SUPPLIER at the SUPPLIER'S expense or make other dispositions as agreed upon by both parties.

(E) If the shipment is specified as 'CIF AMDAHL', then the SUPPLIER shall retain title to the goods, pay shipping costs, and bear the risk of loss or damage until delivery is made to CUSTOMER or the place so designated by CUSTOMER.

(F) If the shipment is specified 'FOB SUPPLIER'S plant', then the SUPPLIER shall bear the cost of delivery of goods to a carrier of the type specified by CUSTOMER. Title to the goods shall pass upon their delivery to the carrier and receipt of the necessary documentation by CUSTOMER.

CUSTOMER shall bear all shipping costs and bear the risk of loss or damage to the goods in transit. Notwithstanding the above, the SUPPLIER shall be liable for any loss or damage discovered after transfer of title which is determined by CUSTOMER to be a result of faulty packaging or handling by the SUPPLIER.

(G) CUSTOMER will not pay for any insurance secured on its behalf by the SUPPLIER.

4. Price

(A) Pricing set forth in Schedule 1 shall be effective for the period up to the first agreed review point. Pricing for each review period thereafter will be mutually agreed upon as a condition of renewal.

(B) Except as set forth in this section and in the section entitled 'Changes', the prices specified after the review point shall remain fixed for all scheduled deliveries unless otherwise agreed in writing by both parties.

(C) SUPPLIER agrees that the prices for the goods or services sold to CUSTOMER are at least as favourable as the prices currently paid by any other customer of SUPPLIER, buying the same or similar goods or services, in equal or smaller quantities, under similar terms and conditions. If during the life of this agreement SUPPLIER reduces the price for any such goods or services to customers of the SUPPLIER for equal or smaller quantities under similar terms and conditions, the SUPPLIER agrees that the corresponding prices under this agreement for goods not yet delivered shall be likewise reduced.

(D) Except as may be otherwise provided in this agreement, the price is exclusive of Government, State, Federal or Local taxes and duties.

5. Terms of payment

(A) The SUPPLIER shall submit invoices to CUSTOMER only upon delivery of goods or completion of services. CUSTOMER shall make payment within forty-five (45) calendar days of receipt of correct invoice and goods, provided the SUPPLIER has delivered conforming goods or satisfactorily completed services.

(B) Adjustments for payments made for rejected goods or services or for any overpayment shall be deducted from payments due or, at CUSTOMER'S discretion, promptly refunded by the SUPPLIER on request.

(C) CUSTOMER shall have the right at any time to set off any amount owing from the SUPPLIER to CUSTOMER or its subsidiaries against any amount payable by CUSTOMER pursuant to this agreement.

6. Indemnification

If the SUPPLIER, its employees, agents or subcontractors enters premises occupied or under the control of CUSTOMER or its customers in the performance of its obligations under this agreement, the SUPPLIER shall indemnify and hold CUSTOMER, its officers, directors, employees and customers harmless from any loss, cost, damage expense or liability by reason of loss, damage or personal injury, of any nature or kind whatsoever, arising out of or as a result of or in connection with such performance or arising out of the negligence of the SUPPLIER, its employees, agents or subcontractors and occasioned in whole or in part by the acts or omissions of the SUPPLIER, its agents, employees, or subcontractors.

In addition, except as specifically provided in this agreement, the SUPPLIER shall indemnify CUSTOMER against any other loss, cost, damage, expense or liability by reason of loss, damage or personal injury, arising out of any performance by the SUPPLIER under this agreement or arising out of any negligence of the SUPPLIER, its employees, agents, or subcontractors and occasioned in whole or in part by the acts or omissions of the SUPPLIER, its agents, employees, or subcontractors.

Evidence of insurance sufficient to meet such indemnities shall be provided to CUSTOMER as a condition of this agreement.

7. Inspection, testing, acceptance and rejection of goods or services

(A) The goods or services to be supplied by the SUPPLIER may be inspected by CUSTOMER at any time prior to delivery. If such inspection takes place on the SUPPLIER'S premises, the SUPPLIER shall provide, at no charge to CUSTOMER, all facilities and assistance required to conduct said inspection. Inspection by CUSTOMER shall not relieve the SUPPLIER of its obligations to deliver goods and services conforming to the requirements of the Agreement.

(B) Acceptance by CUSTOMER of the goods or services to be supplied under this Agreement shall not occur until final inspection and testing in CUSTOMER'S plant. If any goods supplied under this Agreement are found to be non-conforming in material or workmanship, or otherwise not in conformity with the requirements of this Agreement, CUSTOMER may reject and return such goods or services any time within one (1) year after delivery. CUSTOMER may return non-conforming goods to the SUPPLIER at the SUPPLIER'S risk of loss and cost and suspend payment for non-conforming goods or services until such goods or services are made conforming. The SUPPLIER shall bear all risk of loss or damage in connection with rejected goods or services after receiving notice of rejection from CUSTOMER.

(C) The SUPPLIER will provide a Return Material Authorization (RMA) within 24 hours of CUSTOMER'S request, where required to do so by the SUPPLIER.

(D) In the event of CUSTOMER returning non-conforming goods or services to the SUPPLIER, the SUPPLIER shall proceed promptly with the replacement or correction thereof. The SUPPLIER shall not resubmit previously non-conforming goods without prior written approval of CUSTOMER. The SUPPLIER shall identify resubmitted goods as items previously non-conforming.

(E) Payment shall not constitute an acceptance of goods or services nor shall payment impair CUSTOMER'S right to inspect or return non-conforming goods or services or impair any of CUSTOMER'S other remedies (see Section 7 (B) above).

8. Changes

(A) CUSTOMER may at any time make changes within the scope of the Agreement in any of the following areas by written order of its authorized representatives:

    (1) The drawings, designs or specifications for goods to be manufactured under this Agreement;

    (2) The method of shipment or packing;

    (3) The place of delivery, inspection or acceptance.

(B) Only CUSTOMER'S technical representatives may exchange technical information with the SUPPLIER'S technical representatives. Any such exchange of information shall be undertaken for the sole purpose of assisting the SUPPLIER to perform its obligations under this Agreement. Such exchange shall not be considered changes unless documented as part of the change procedure set forth in Section 8 (A) above.

(C) If any change affects the time for or the cost of performance under this Agreement, or otherwise materially affects any provisions of the Agreement, an equitable adjustment shall be negotiated in the price or delivery schedule, or both, and in such other provisions of the Agreement as may be affected. Such adjustment shall be accompanied by a written amendment to the Agreement and signed by a representative of CUSTOMER. Any claim for adjustment under this section must be made by the SUPPLIER within thirty (30) days after receipt of the written order set out in Section 8 (A) above.

(D) In all cases, the SUPPLIER shall proceed with performance of the Agreement as changed.

9. Compliance with laws and regulations

The SUPPLIER shall comply with all applicable laws and regulations.

10. Warranty

(A) The SUPPLIER warrants that all goods delivered hereunder shall be (1) free of all defects whether of materials or workmanship or otherwise, (2) in accordance with all specifications, models, samples and descriptions relating thereto, (3) if designed by the Supplier free from defects in design and (4) free of all claims, liens and encumbrances.

(B) CUSTOMER shall be entitled to rely on the said and any other warranties of the SUPPLIER notwithstanding that CUSTOMER may have inspected, tested, accepted or paid for the goods and all such warranties shall endure for the benefit of CUSTOMER, its successors and assigns.

(C) The SUPPLIER'S obligation under this warranty is limited to at CUSTOMER'S option:

   (1) Performing services to CUSTOMER'S satisfaction; or
   (2) Repairing or replacing non-conforming goods within 48 hours of notice of non-conformance; or
   (3) Crediting or refunding to CUSTOMER the purchase price of such goods or services.

   All expenses associated with the return to the SUPPLIER of non-conforming goods and the delivery to CUSTOMER of repaired or replacement goods shall be borne by the SUPPLIER.

(D) The term of warranty shall be one (1) year from date of receipt at CUSTOMER.

11. Confidential information and rights to ideas

(A) The SUPPLIER acknowledges that all information, data, material and things concerning CUSTOMER or its affairs which come to its knowledge in connection with this Agreement or its past and future relationship with CUSTOMER are entirely confidential ('confidential information').

(B) Confidential information includes in particular (without limiting the generality of the foregoing):

   (1) The fact of this Agreement and the relationship it creates;
   (2) The terms and operation of this Agreement;
   (3) Any information in any medium supplied by CUSTOMER, or for which CUSTOMER is charged or in any way related to the business and affairs of CUSTOMER;

   but does not include information which is or becomes through no fault of the SUPPLIER in the public domain.

(C) The SUPPLIER agrees that it will at all times:

   (1) Keep all confidential information entirely safe, secure, confidential and properly maintained and insured;

    (2) Not disclose any confidential information except to its employees where necessary to comply with its obligations hereunder;

    (3) Not make use of any confidential information unless and to the extent necessary to comply with its obligations hereunder;

    (4) Not copy or reproduce or convert any confidential information;

    (5) Immediately upon request by CUSTOMER or immediately upon termination of this Agreement for whatever reason, return at its own cost all confidential information to CUSTOMER;

    (6) Indemnify CUSTOMER for any consequences of breach by the SUPPLIER or its employees of the terms of this clause, whether or not the SUPPLIER is responsible for such breach.

(D) The SUPPLIER shall not, without CUSTOMER'S prior written permission, advertise or otherwise disclose the fact that it has furnished or agreed to furnish goods or services to CUSTOMER under the Agreement. The SUPPLIER agrees not to disclose or discuss with third parties the content, terms or conditions of this Agreement without CUSTOMER'S prior written permission.

12. Patent, copyright and intellectual property matters

(A) The SUPPLIER shall settle or defend, at its sole expense, including the payment of all costs and damages awarded, any claim against CUSTOMER, its subsidiaries, affiliates, and their respective customers alleging that goods, or any part or item thereof, furnished under this Agreement, or any use thereof, infringes any patent, copyright, trademark, trade secret or other intellectual property interest now or hereafter. The SUPPLIER shall promptly notify Amdahl of any such claim.

(B) CUSTOMER may participate in any such proceedings at its own expense.

(C) CUSTOMER shall hold the SUPPLIER harmless against any expense or loss resulting from any infringements of any patent or trade mark due to compliance with designs or specifications supplied by CUSTOMER to the SUPPLIER.

(D) If a final injunction against CUSTOMER'S use of goods results from such a claim, or if CUSTOMER reasonably believes such a claim is likely, the SUPPLIER shall, at its own expense, and as CUSTOMER requests, obtain for CUSTOMER the right to continue using the goods or replace or modify the goods so they become non-infringing but remain functionally equivalent.

13. Assignment

(A) Neither the Agreement nor the right or obligation thereunder may be assigned or delegated by the SUPPLIER without the prior written consent of CUSTOMER. Any attempt to assign or delegate contrary to the provisions of this section is void and will have no effect.

(B) The SUPPLIER agrees that it will not subcontract for completed or substantially completed goods or major components for supply to CUSTOMER without the prior consent of CUSTOMER.

14. Unauthorised changes

This Agreement is made with the SUPPLIER and accepted by him on the express condition that the SUPPLIER shall make no change in any design, configuration, material, part or manufacturing process which has been approved by CUSTOMER and applicable to this Agreement without the prior written permission of CUSTOMER.

15. General

(A) No term or condition in this Agreement shall be deemed waived by CUSTOMER and no breach excused unless such waiver or consent is received in writing and signed by an authorized CUSTOMER representative. No consent by CUSTOMER to, or waiver of, a breach by the SUPPLIER, whether express or implied, shall constitute a consent to, waiver of, or excuse for any other different or subsequent breach by the SUPPLIER.

(B) Notwithstanding anything else in the Agreement, no default, delay or failure to perform on the part of either party shall be chargeable hereunder if such default, delay or failure to perform is due to causes beyond the reasonable control of the party so affected. In the event of any such default, delay or failure to perform, any dates or times by which the party is otherwise scheduled to perform shall be extended automatically for a period of time equal in duration to the time the cause for such default, delay or failure to perform was in effect.

(C) The Supplier shall not make or offer a gratuity or gift of any kind to CUSTOMER employees or their families. CUSTOMER will interpret any such gratuity or gift as an improper attempt to influence CUSTOMER'S employees.

(D) The SUPPLIER shall take all necessary actions to prevent situations which are, or may give the appearance of being, a conflict of interest in connection with or in any way, related to its relationship with CUSTOMER.

(E) If any term or condition of this Agreement shall be found to be illegal or unenforceable, such term or provision shall be deemed stricken and all other terms and conditions of the Agreement shall remain in full force and effect.

(F) Headings used in the Agreement are for convenience only and are not to be used to interpret the Agreement between both parties.

(G) Any notices required or permitted to be given pursuant to this Agreement shall be in writing and shall be deemed to have been given when received.

(H) This Agreement and all attachments hereto constitutes the entire understanding between CUSTOMER and the SUPPLIER with respect to the purchase of the specified goods and services and supersedes all prior oral and written communications. This Agreement may be amended or modified only in writing signed by authorized representatives of both parties.

(I) The Agreement and these conditions shall be governed by and construed in accordance with the laws of Ireland and it is hereby irrevocably agreed for the exclusive benefit of CUSTOMER that the Courts of Ireland are to have jurisdiction to settle any disputes which may arise out of or in connection with the Agreement and these conditions and that accordingly a suit, action or proceeding arising out of or in connection with the Agreement and these conditions (in this clause referred to as 'proceedings') may be brought in such Courts.

16. Reservation of title

Notwithstanding delivery, the goods sold hereunder shall remain the absolute property of the SUPPLIER until payment of all monies due and payable by CUSTOMER to the SUPPLIER and outstanding from time to time have been paid. CUSTOMER agree to store all goods supplied by the SUPPLIER in such a way that they are readily identifiable as his property.

Customs, Excise and VAT

The introduction of the Single European Market signalled the abolition of customs checks at internal EC frontiers, so that most goods moving between member states are no longer subject to customs documents or procedures.

The main changes are:

- Goods in free circulation, that is, community goods and third country goods in respect of which import duties have been paid, being traded between member states will no longer have to be covered by a Customs Declaration at import or export points, nor will these goods have to be presented to 'Customs'. Spot checks for illicit goods, such as drugs or other threats to society, may continue to be carried out, but these checks will be selective and geared to avoid interfering with the flow of trade.

- Goods not in free circulation will continue to move between member states under external Community transit (T1) arrangements, but goods which are in free circulation will not, with limited exceptions, have to be covered by a transit procedure.
- VAT on imports from the EC countries will no longer be collected at point of entry. VAT registered persons will, however, be required to account in their normal VAT returns by declaring liability for such imports and taking an input credit, or deduction if appropriate.
- As at present, excise duties will, in general, continue to be payable in the country of consumption at the rates of that country. New control systems, not based on border checks, and import–export documentation have been introduced for that purpose.

Customs documentation will be used for imports from and exports to non-member states of the EC and, in addition, goods which are not in free circulation will continue to be placed under the external Community transit (T1) procedure when moving between member states.

It is no longer necessary to present import and export declarations (on SAD forms) for Community goods moving from one member state to another.

Transit passengers on board an aircraft arriving from a third country (e.g. United States), which calls at one Community airport (e.g. London) and continues its journey to another Community airport (e.g. Milan), will have their cabin and hold baggage checked by Customs at the airport of final destination (i.e. Milan). Community passengers joining the flight at the first Community airport will also be liable to customs checks on arrival at the second Community airport, to avoid collusion.

As regards transfer passengers arriving on an aircraft from a third country who disembark at the first Community airport (e.g. London) and continue their journey on a different aircraft to a second Community airport (e.g. Milan) the normal rule will be that they will have their hand luggage checked at the first airport (i.e. London) and their hold luggage will not be checked by Customs until they arrive at the final airport (i.e. Milan).

In principle, goods arriving direct from another EC port or airport will be assumed to be Community goods (with no requirement to prove status) unless there is evidence to the contrary.

Duty-free sales and EC travel after 1992

The sale of duty-free goods to passengers making intra-EC ferry crossings and taking intra-EC flights will continue to be permitted until 30 June 1999. Thereafter, it is envisaged that this concession will no longer be available to the intra-Community traveller.

The continuation of duty-free sales after 1992 will not, however, entail customs checks on travellers arriving at ports and airports. Because of trade in illicit goods such as drugs, firearms and explosives, frontier checks will not disappear entirely. Such checks will, however, take account of the expectation of business and individuals for free movement within the European Community and will be carried out in a manner which is unobtrusive, selective and highly targeted on traffic of greater risk.

Excise duty-suspended goods

All production, processing and holding of excisable goods on which excise duty has not been paid must take place in an authorized warehouse. The authorization system incorporates many of the control procedures, including a requirement for a financial guarantee related to potential duty liability, that applies under the existing national excise warehousing regime. Most bonded warehouses qualifying under the old system qualify for authorization under the new system.

Movement of duty-suspended goods between member states will always originate in an authorized warehouse. The goods may move to:

- another authorized warehouse,
- a registered trader, or
- a non-registered trader.

Registered traders are required to:

- provide a financial guarantee to cover liability for the excise duty,
- keep accounts and produce the goods for examination whenever so required,
- consent to control and stock checks, and
- pay duty on receipt of the goods.

Non-registered traders wishing to engage in intra-Community duty-suspended trade are required to:

- make prior declaration to their fiscal authorities and guarantee the excise duty in advance of the dispatch of the goods,
- consent to any checks prescribed, and
- pay duty at the time of receipt of the goods.

The financial guarantee in the case of registered traders is a general guarantee related *inter alia* to the anticipated volume of activity in a particular period while that for non-registered traders will generally be transaction-related.

All intra-Community movement of duty-suspended excisable goods is covered by an accompanying document issued by the authorized warehousekeeper of dispatch. This is a single document with provision for up to five copies. It constitutes the key control mechanism for fiscal authorities. The various copies of the accompanying document are disposed of as follows:

- Copy 1 – will be retained by the consignor (the authorized warehousekeeper of dispatch).
- Copy 2 – will be retained by the consignee.
- Copy 3 – will travel with the goods.
- Copy 4 – will be given to the fiscal authorities of the member state of destination.
- Copy 5 – may be requested by the fiscal authorities of the member state of dispatch.

A particular transaction (and the liability of the consignor) will be discharged when copy 3 is returned to the consignor indicating receipt of the goods. However, a member state may require that the accompanying document be stamped by it.

In cases where the consignee is a non-registered trader, there will be a need for a further document certifying that excise duty has, for instance, been paid or secured in the member state of destination.

Excise duty paid goods

Duty paid goods moved for commercial purpose from one member state to another are subject to excise duty in the latter member state and at the rates applying in that member state. There is provision for reimbursement of the duty paid in the first member state. Those involved in such trade must:

- Make prior declaration to their fiscal authorities and guarantee the excise duty in advance of dispatch of the goods.
- Consent to any checks prescribed.
- Pay the excise duty in accordance with the procedure laid down by their member state.

Movement of duty paid goods between member states takes place under cover of a simplified accompanying document drawn up by the person responsible for the movement.

Private transactions

With the exception of hydrocarbon oils and motor vehicles, goods acquired in another member state by private individuals for their own use and carried by them when returning to their own member state are not subject to further duty on their return. Criteria have been laid down to enable private transactions to be distinguished from commercial transactions. These include the commercial status of the holder of the goods as well as the quantity carried. Indicative limits have been set in relation to quantity in the case of alcoholic beverages and tobacco products. If these are exceeded, there would then be an onus on the person carrying out the transaction to prove that it was a private one.

Excise duties

Excise duties on alcoholic drinks, tobacco products and mineral oils continue after 1993. Other excise duties may not depend for their operation on border controls. In this context, alternative methods of taxing motor vehicles have been decided.

Excise duty continues to be payable at the rate of duty in, and to the administration of, the country of consumption. The only important exception will be purchases by travellers for private purposes. To achieve this a minimum system of Community actions has been introduced, leaving it to member states to supplement this with national controls as their circumstances require. The new system applies to alcoholic beverages, mineral oils and tobacco products.

There is an EC-wide systems of authorized bonded warehouses and registered operators. Duty is due when goods leave the warehouse system, or, in the case of registered operators, on their receipt. Traders who are neither registered nor part of the warehouse network may also receive consignments of excisable goods, provided they notify their fiscal authority and secure the duty in advance of receipt.

There are requirements for an accompanying document, administrative or commercial, to be used by excise traders to confirm receipt of the goods. Member states are also entitled to maintain or introduce taxes on other products provided such taxes do not involve the use of frontier controls.

VAT

The new rules for VAT in inter-member state trade have applied from 1 January 1993 (Council Directive 91/680/EEC(1) Directive (2)).

The new rules will be in force until at least 1 January 1997 when a change is expected. Up to 1997, cross-frontier sales between most business operators will be taxed in the hands of the purchaser in the country of destination of goods; and after 1997 such sales will be taxed in the hands of the seller in the country of origin, if agreement is reached by parliaments and Council.

From 1 January 1993 there has been no VAT charge at importation between member states. The three basic types of transaction in the post-1993 system are:

- Sales from business to business.
- Sales to operators not liable for VAT on their sales.
- Sales to individuals.

Sales from business to business, VAT-exempt companies and individuals

The seller can supply goods at zero rate on supplies he makes to customers in other member states, subject to two conditions: the goods must physically go from one member state to another, and the customer must be registered for VAT. From this it can be seen that the purchaser has to advise the seller of his VAT registration number.

The seller completes his normal periodic VAT return showing in a separate box the total of his exempted intra-community sales, and sends details, on a quarterly basis of the VAT numbers of his customers in other member states together with the total value of his sales to each of them during the period.

The invoice raised for each transaction must show the supplier's VAT number and that of the customer.

The purchaser is liable to VAT on his acquisition and declares the total of such acquisitions in a separate box on the VAT return and claims a deduction for the VAT in the same return.

Purchases from small VAT-exempt companies will not give rise to VAT on acquisition and services generally continue to be treated as before but new rules have been introduced for intra-EC transport services.

Individuals travelling from one member state to another to buy goods will pay VAT where they buy the goods and will not be liable to VAT when they return to their own member state. They are the same as if they were residents of the member state where the purchase is made. Individuals moving residence or travelling with items for their personal use, or gifts, are not subject to any further VAT charge nor to any border formalities when they cross from one member state to another.

The purchase of a new car by an individual will be taxed in the country of destination, which will as a general rule be the country in which the car is registered for road use. VAT on acquisition will be collected at the time of registration. Goods which are imported from non-EC countries are liable for VAT at importation.

Goods exported to non-EC countries are exempt from VAT.

The harmonizing action of VAT rates has begun. As of the 1 January 1993 the general rule is that a rates system should include a standard rate at 15 per cent and, should the member states require it, one or two reduced rates of at least 5 per cent. There are several exceptions, such as in the case of distance selling, that is mail order by private individuals, when VAT, subject to a threshold, will be chargeable at the rate applicable in the member state of the customer.

Other EC Programmes

These are programmes of possible interest not already covered in the main Framework programme and other industrial and commercial programmes. Unlike those detailed in Chapters 9, 10 and 25, they cannot be directly negotiated with the EC, as they are administered through national governments.

Here are the broad categories:

1. Education and further education.
2. Pilot projects and demonstration projects.
3. Coal and steel research.
4. Innovation and technology transfer.
5. Regional promotion of technological infrastructures.
6. Data and information transmission.

It is important to note that these can, unlike Framework, be at market-ready stage.

1. Education and further education

Two programmes in this category, ERASMUS and LINGUA, deal with students and teachers, and are not discussed here. Another, TEMPOS, is a mobility programme for the universities of central and eastern Europe, while another, ACE, is for exchanges between economists in the same area, and COMETT II is for education and training for technology.

COMETT II

This programme is also discussed in Chapter 25 and serves to promote cooperation between universities and industry in training in advanced technology, especially in response to technological change. It is aimed at those who have completed their initial training and at those in active employment. It is worth ECU 200 million and the specific areas supported are:

- The development and establishment of partnerships in the field of education between universities and business.
- Cross-border interchange of students and university graduates, scientists and specialists.
- Projects to promote continuing training in the technology sector and multimedia distance education.
- Supplementary and associated initiatives.

2. Pilot projects and demonstration programmes

There is only one current project of interest. This is THERMIE, a very important industrially-relevant programme on new energy technologies. Considerable financial risk must be involved on the part of the researcher making the application for the grant. It is worth ECU 35 million and the programme supports the following activities.

- National use of energy, energy savings in buildings and industry, power generation, distribution, energy savings in transport and urban infrastructure.
- All renewable energy sources; solid fuels; environmentally benign techniques; hydrocarbons, exploration, exploitation, transport, storage.

3. Coal and steel research

The EC promotes technical and scientific research aimed at increasing the use of coal and steel, as well as operational safety in these industries. Support is given to projects initiated by enterprises, research institutes or individuals. Applications must be submitted before 1 September each year for the following year. The areas concerned may be listed under four main headings.

Technical coal research (ECSC) 1990–1995

- Mining technology, including advance work and support systems, engineering, firedamp, ventilation, extraction, infrastructure, management technology.
- Product upgrading, including processing, metallurgical use, upgrading and converting coal.

Technical steel research (ECSC) 1991–1995

- Improving quality and reducing costs.
- Sale and new markets.
- Meeting environmental demands in production.

Medical research (ECSC)

By 1994 a sixth five year programme should have emerged. The fifth, ending in 1992, dealt with the protection of workers against the dangers of the workplace in the coal mining and the iron and steel industries. Areas of research included occupation-related illnesses. It was worth ECU 12 million.

Social research (ECSC) 1990–1994

This sixth programme deals with safety in the development and introduction of new technologies, reduction of major health risks, improved general working and environmental conditions. It has four sections: ergonomics safety, health and the combatting of environmental nuisance, worth between them ECU 89 million. The last, combatting environmental nuisance, finished in 1992, but may repeat in this or another form.

4. Innovation and technology transfer

Two programmes are of interest in this category, both finished or finishing. The first, SPRINT, should repeat in this or another form. It finished in 1993 and was worth ECU 90 million. It was aimed at promoting the dissemination of new technologies and innovations by integrating national innovation infrastructures into a European network, and by promoting specific projects and coordinating and monitoring national innovation.

This programme has been aimed at public and private consultancy bodies who represented SMEs and partners from other states, particularly for technology transfer. It even included the promotion of information seminars, exhibitions, technology fairs and so on. Further developments of SPRINT should be watched with interest.

The second programme, NETT, has been set up as a network for environmental technology transfer. No further call for proposals existed at the time of writing, but the network itself may be of interest. It has three services, which are:

- DATANETT. An online data bank of environmental standards and regulations, markets for environmental technologies, programmes of support, including EC funding.
- Research and development service. Advice to NETT members, including help in searching for partners and financial support.
- Meetings service. The organization of meetings, seminars, trade fairs.

5. Regional promotion of technological infrastructures

One of the better known promotions, finished in 1991, was STAR, which offered telecommunications facilities to less advantaged regions. Since 1991, one spin-off has been the Telamatique programme, which called for proposals on how to use the kind of facilities implemented under STAR.

STAR was large, worth ECU 1,500 million, of which the ERDF, the European Regional Development Fund contributed ECU 750 million. This area should be watched for further developments.

A second programme in this category and also finishing is STRIDE, worth ECU 400 million which promotes both the strengthening of research facilities in regions lagging behind in communications and the interconnection and linkages between research centres and industry. More developments are expected.

6. Data and information transmissions

There are two programmes of interest in this category. The first is IMPACT II, 1991–1995, worth ECU 100 million, which aims to establish a single market in information services. It also promotes research into advanced information services, and wants to stimulate and strengthen the competitiveness of European sellers of information services.

The second programme, discussed in Chapter 23, is TEDIS II, 1991–1994, worth ECU 25 million, 15 million of which will be spent in 1993 and 1994. The title of this programme is 'Trade Electronic Data Interchange System', and its aims are to develop electronic data systems for trade, industry and administration. It fits in with other programmes.

Outside the Community

Finally, in the area of programme funding, the EC has a programme of international scientific cooperation, promoting cooperation between laboratories in the European Community and those in other countries, in South and Central America, the Gulf, Israel, Yugoslavia, Bangladesh, Brunei, China, Philippines, India, Indonesia, Malaysia, Pakistan, Qatar, Singapore, Sri Lanka, Thailand, and Yemen.

It sponsors joint research projects, and finances visiting scientists to Europe. It will also support workshops and promote personal contacts.

Index

Advanced manufacturing
technology 103–4

Banking facilities 221–7
economic information
service 223
exchange rate services 226
export finance 225–6
foreign currency accounts 223–5
international money transfer
services 224–5
letters of credit 227
trade development service
222–3
BC-NET (Business Cooperation
Network) 205–6
BIC (Business Innovation
Centre) 206–7

Border controls 14
BRE 208
BRITE/EURAM 76–8, 90–93, 208
BS 7750 23, 108, 121, 145, 151, 169,
198

CE Mark 24, 121, 129, 195
CEN 22, 125
Certification 193–204
products and processes
needing 127
Citizenship 8–15
COMETT II 209, 254
Compulsory standards 127–8
Computer integrated
manufacturing 104
Construction Products
Directive 197

Consumer protection 133–8
COST 210
Customs 246–52

EC directives,
    products covered by 123
EC Eco-audit Regulation 22, 23,
    121, 130, 150–59
EC grants 67–81, 88–98
    bursaries and subsidies 71
    Framework 68–9, 75
    model contract 74
    research 70–71
EC market for services 62–6
Economic and Monetary Union
    26–30
    the UK position 29
EC Packaging Waste Directive 166
EC Programmes 68–81, 253–7
    agriculture 79, 89, 220
    AIM 76
    biomedical/health research 79, 89
    BIOMED I 89
    biotechnology 78
    BRITE/EURAM 76–7, 90–91, 208
    coal and steel research 255
    COMETT II 254, 209
    communications 76, 96
    data and information
        transmissions 257
    DATANETT 256
    DELTA 76
    development of statistical expert
        systems 91–2
    DOSES II 91–2
    DRA 76
    DRIVE 76
    education 254
    EEAGF 220
    employment creation 219
    energies, non-nuclear 80, 96
    environment 77
    environmental R&D
        programme 92
    ESPRIT 75, 92
    ETP 213
    EUREKA 92–3
    EURET 93–4

Euromanagement 94
EUROTECHNET II 214
FORCE 215
Framework 75–81
    human capital and mobility
        80–81, 94
    IBC 76
    IMPACT II 94–5, 257
    industrial and materials
        technologies 76–7
    industrial R&D initiative 95
    information technology 75
    innovation and technology
        transfer 256
    INTERPRISE 215
    IRIS 215–16
    knowledge, dissemination and
        exploitation of 81
    LEI 95
    life sciences for developing
        countries 79–80, 216
    LINGUA 216
    marine science 78
    measurement and testing 77
    MEDIA 96
    NETT 256
    nuclear 80
    partnerships 215
    PETRA 13, 98
    pilot projects 254
    RACE II 96
    regional promotion of technology
        transfer 256–7
    SAVE 97
    small and community
        enterprises 218
    SPEC 219
    SPRINT 97, 256
    TEDIS II 97–8, 189–92, 257
    telematics 76, 98
    THERMIE 98, 254
    transport 93–4
    venture consort scheme 217–18
    vocational training 214–15
    women 96, 215–16
ECU 28
EC VDT regulation 170
EDI 97–9, 105–6, 189–92